SWIMMING IS

by
LEN SHEARN

illustrated by
J.E.B.

ABSON BOOKS, Abson, Wick, Bristol

First published in Great Britain in 1982
by ABSON BOOKS, Abson, Wick, Bristol.

© Len Shearn

All rights reserved. No part of this publication may be reproduced, stored in a retrieval system or transmitted in any form, by any means, without prior permission of the publishers.

ISBN 0 902920 49 9

Printed and bound at K.B. Printing Services, 149 Mina Road, Bristol BS2 9YQ, England.

Preface

This book is intended to appeal in the main to the beginner, and to those who have progressed a little way along the path to achievement.

It is with great pleasure that I welcome you to the company of Jenny and Jimmy, so that with them you may splutter and splash, puff and blow, and finally reach the realms of accomplishment.

L. SHEARN

Advanced Teacher & Examiner,
Amateur Swimming Association.

Service Cross, 1st class Instructor and
Examiner, Royal Life Saving Society.

Examiner-Instructor,
Swimming Teachers' Association.

Foreword

I have known Len Shearn for many years, his achievements in helping and obtaining success for the timid and handicapped children and adults are known and appreciated throughout the community.

The photograph on Page 5 is of myself with the 'Sportsman of the Year Trophy' and Len with the 'Silver Salver' in recognition of his many years of devoted service to the teaching of swimming.

The trophies were presented to us at the Sportsman's Dinner at the Redwood Lodge Country Club, Bristol, so it gives me great pleasure to be associated with Len and to wish him every success with his book 'SWIMMING IS FUN'.

Robin Cousins
MBE

Robin Cousins

Contents

	Page
General Introduction	7
Snips from my memoirs	10
The First Lesson	17
The Front Crawl	20
The Back Crawl	28
The Breast Stroke	35
The Back Stroke or Life Saving Stroke	41
Jumping into the water and treading water	44
Diving	47
Rescue Methods	57
Resuscitation	58
A.S.A. Swimming Awards	63
Swimming Stunts	65
B.S.C.A. Swimming Awards	68
R.L.S.S. The Blue Code	72

GENERAL INFORMATION

"Can anyone learn to swim? And how do I set about it?"

These are two questions I have been asked many times. My answer to the first is "yes". The second I will endeavour to answer as, with Jimmy and Jenny, we follow all the ways to learn.

In the first place, we must remember the three main factors which cause us to sink in water. They are:

(1) Bone structure
(2) Muscle tension
(3) Lack of air in the body

We cannot do anything about No.1. because that is how we are made, but we can do something about No.2. by relaxing the muscles, and about No.3. by learning how to breathe correctly in the water.

The majority of women, for example, will float naturally because of their relaxed muscles, which give them natural buoyancy, whereas a man finds it very difficult to keep afloat. His legs will nearly always sink because of muscle tension, and of holding the breath. Therefore, we must acquire, above everything else, relaxation of the muscles and natural breathing.

SWIMMING IS FUN

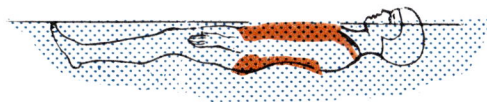

Jenny floating   (Fig.1.)

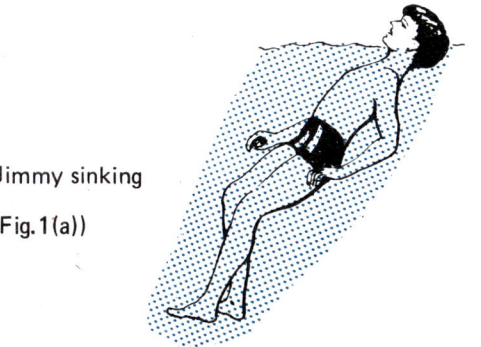

Jimmy sinking

(Fig.1(a))

Swimming comes naturally to some, and others find it most difficult. In everybody, however, is implanted an instinct which tells them how to kick their legs and use their arms.

For example, one will either use a natural breast stroke or front crawl action, while another will feel more happy and confident using the back stroke action. One should use whichever stroke comes naturally, and so gain confidence in that stroke first.

You would not dream of teaching a cricketer or tennis player who is naturally left-handed to play right-handed. If a person writes with the left hand, you don't insist on using the right. The same principle applies in learning to swim. Do that which is comfortable and natural, whether it be front crawl, breast stroke, or swimming on the back. Encourage the natural tendencies first, and you will be going with the tide instead of across it.

Inflatable arm bands and foam floats, which can be obtained from dealers in sports equipment, will prove to be a great help. They are shown in Fig.2.

The foam float, made from expanded polystyrene, is an absolute "must" if you are to perfect the leg action of any stroke, for the leg action is the basis of all successful swimming.

(Fig.2.)
Arm bands and floats

Personally I favour arm bands as swimming aids, as they are easy to carry and when inflated, enable you to float on the water. This allows your arms and legs to do the swimming strokes, but above all, they give lots of confidence to the beginner. (see Fig.3.)

Another simple aid to confidence, (particularly young children) is to give them a Table Tennis ball to blow along in front of them. This will cause them to concentrate on blowing the ball and incidentally to automatically do the "Dog Paddle" to get to the ball, and also to lose the fear of putting their faces into the water and breathing out. (See Fig.4.)

I do not, however, decry the use of any kind of aid so long as confidence is thereby encouraged, for that is the foundation on which all swimming strokes are based. When confidence to lie forward or backward on the water has been once acquired, the strokes will follow. With confidence comes relaxation, and allowing one's self time to think.

In this book I have purposely given each stroke a separate chapter, so that you may readily refer to any of the strokes at any time.

I would, however, at this point, like to tell one or two true stories from my "Book of Memoirs" in order to illustrate my "method" and to prove that no barrier is insurmountable. Also, that success can be both achieved and deserved.

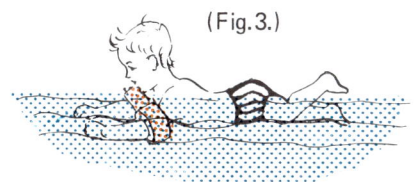

(Fig.3.)

(Fig.4.)

Inflated arm bands to help beginners to float & swim.

SNIPS FROM MY MEMOIRS

THE STORY OF ANDREW AND HIS BROTHER...

The parents of a boy named Andrew, aged seven, came to me because of their very serious concern for him. Andrew was born deaf and dumb, and was also spastic. His leg muscles were limited, which caused him difficulty in the normal use of his legs. To add to his parents' worry, they lived near a big river, and Andrew was keen on playing near and with water. His mother told me she was terrified lest he followed his playmates into the river, and, being unable to call for help, would simply drown.

Here was a problem, and a challenge to my "method".

He was a delightful little chap. I took him to the shallow end of the bath and watched his attempts to imitate what the other children were doing. It was obvious that he could not go forward on his tummy because of the weakness in his legs. I tried him floating on his back, and found he was quite buoyant. I decided to teach him the "sculling" movement and the back crawl first. I would show him the movement, and then, by holding his arms and legs, would manipulate them in the way I wanted him to use them.

Within a few weeks he was able to "scull" across the bath, and to do the "flutter kick" on his back without assistance. From this I put him into the back crawl, which he acquired fairly easily. From this I got him using the float on the front, then the "dog paddle", and finally the front crawl.

The letter I received from his father is reproduced here.

---

68 Arbutus Drive,
Bristol 9
15/6/66.

My wife & I were very worried regarding our son Andrew who is aged seven years. He is severely deaf with very little speech & was also born a spastic with lack of control in his walking, arm movement, & sense of balance.

We also live near the River Avon which caused us much anxiety as Andrew & his brother loves the water, we also play about in boats so naturally our fears for him were ever present.

Mr. Shearn took him for swimming lessons as a challenge to his way of teaching & as a result after less than 2 years, Andrew can dive, swim front crawl & back crawl in any depth of water.

We also have found that swimming has helped immensely to help coordinate his muscle movement so that today his movements are almost normal.

Naturally my wife & I are delighted with his progress & shall ever be grateful to swimming, which besides giving Andrew immense joy & pleasure, also affords him the satisfaction of being able to do the same as other boys & girls.

Sydney W. Harris

Today he swims and dives with complete confidence. He is able to do what other children can do in the swimming bath, and just lives for that alone. Above all, the swimming has been so beneficial that his leg muscles are now greatly developed, and he is able to walk and run without stumbling or falling. Andrew, with maximum support from his family, was so dedicated to swimming that he won numerous awards and at the age of 16 years won the National 100 metres Back Stroke Championships for the deaf, also the 100 metres Free Style Championship, and eventually in Kapsovar, Hungary, beat the Russian holder and won the European 200 metres Back Stroke Championship for the deaf. The appended photograph shows Andrew with the Championship trophies together with his gold medal. (See opposite).

THE BOY WHO DREADED SWIMMING LESSONS

Two parents came to me who were extremely worried over their boy, aged fourteen.

He was afraid of water, and every time the school had a swimming lesson he would work himself up into a dreadful state, often coming out in a rash. As a result his school work deteriorated.

I went into the bath and just walked around with him, chatting as we walked. He told me that every time he went to the baths the other boys would make fun of him because he was afraid of the water. It was clear that his was a psychological problem.

I had him walking around in the water up to his armpits, and occasionally got him to put his face in the water. I then put a weighted block of wood about 3" square on the bottom of the bath, and asked him to try to pick it up. This gave him something to concentrate on, and at the same time caused him to put his head into the water, creating confidence and helping to allay his fear of water. Then, by using the floats, I got him gliding gradually to the bar.

He was scared every time the water splashed into his face. It was useless trying to teach him anything other than the breast stroke to begin with, as in this stroke the water is not so liable to splash. Also, his legs and body were so dreadfully tensed that it would have been difficult to try any other stroke.

However, by the continual practise of holding the rail, pulling himself to it, and using the float, he gradually acquired confidence.

From this, I got him holding the bar and doing the breast stroke leg movement, then the same by holding the float. The bending of the knees made him relax, and, gradually, as he gained confidence, he relaxed completely, and in a matter of weeks he was able to swim.

As a consequence, the rash disappeared, his school work improved, and he was a changed boy.

IF YOO CAN SWIMM HOO KNEEDS TO SPEL?

Club swimming coach Len Shearn catches them young. And he also gets some charming letters of thanks from his pupils.

When he recently sent a 20 metre swimming badge and certificate to a 4-year-old swimmer Lisa McWilliams . . he also sent a "get well" card as he had heard she was sick.

This was the reply he received:

It is such a gem of a letter that we feel it should be shown.

"Dear Mistr Sheern
thank yoo for my lovlee kard and
a my sertif
ikate
love Lisa"

SUSAN...

A little girl named Susan, aged nine, had lost the use of her right arm due to polio. Although many kinds of treatment had been tried, her arm remained useless.

First I taught her how to lie on her back in the water in the floating position, and then to flick her legs up and down. At the same time I taught her to use her good arm with the sculling movement, whilst I manipulated the other arm in the same way.

In time I began to feel movement returning to her arm, and after many months of patience and practice, Susan regained a good 50 per cent of movement. Above all, she was able to swim quite well, and eventually obtained swimming and life-saving awards.

The moral here is that handicaps are no bar to learning to swim.

IT'S NEVER TOO LATE...

A lady aged sixty-three years had always wanted to swim, but was terrified to relinquish her hold of the bath rail. The slightest splash in her face would cause her to throw her head back and panic. I got her to put her toes under the rail, lie back on the water and just breathe, breathe, breathe.

At first she was very tensed, but gradually she was able to relax. From this we went into the floating and kicking with and without the foam float, and eventually into the back crawl.

Now, at the age of sixty-five, she is able to swim many lengths on the back crawl, and thoroughly enjoys every minute. She can also use the front crawl a little, but with nothing like the same confidence. The reason: it is **natural** for her to swim on her back, and swimming takes no account of age.

FINE FEATHERS...

At the swimming baths in a poor quarter of the city one day, a little boy of about eight years came up to me. Tapping me on the leg, he said "Hey mister, there's a kid down there (pointing to the deep end) and he can't 'alf 'old his breff a long time".

I went to the deep end, and sure enough at the bottom of the steps leading into the water was a boy.

I brought him to the surface, and artificial respiration was successfully applied. In the meantime, someone had informed the Superintendent of the Bath, who came hurriedly in.

The boy was now conscious, but sobbing, and it was noticed that he **was** wearing swimming trunks much too large for him, supported by a **belt**. On the swimming trunks was a life-saving badge.

"Can you swim?" asked the Superintendent. "No, sir," replied the boy. "Then why," demanded the Superintendent "are you wearing that life-saving badge on your swimming trunks?".

"These ain't mine, "replied the boy. "They're me bruvver's".

The moral here is: Keep away from the deep end if you can't swim, don't wear badges to which you are not entitled; fine feathers don't make fine birds.

Jenny and Jim entering baths

And now, with Jimmy and Jenny, let us head for the starting post for the "off".

RECOMMENDATIONS

I am pleased to introduce the author of this book to you. I have known Mr. Len Shearn personally for nearly twenty years, and I am pleased to have this opportunity of recommending a book which has been written for the beginner. Very few Swimming books are written for the child in the process of learning such a worthwhile skill as Swimming.

You can enjoy reading not only about learning to swim, but also starting to Dive, Life-saving, and Synchronised swimming. You might well imagine yourself as one of the characters in this book.

Len Shearn must be thought of by many hundreds of past and present pupils with affection and gratitude. His experience and love of children is evident, and he has presented his thoughts which after many years of teaching he finds provides success quickly.

The title is very apt, and if you cannot swim yet, why not learn now? 'Swimming is fun'.

Helen J. Elkington

Lecturer Bedford College,
F.I.S.T. & F.I.S.C. Institute of Swimming Teachers and Coaches

I have often watched Mr. Shearn giving my children and other children swimming lessons, they obviously enjoy every minute of it and apart from teaching well he makes it tremendous fun for them; somehow he manages to give them a great deal of confidence.

Confidence to my mind is a necessity in being taught to swim — Mr. Shearn is certainly an artist in giving this to his pupils. He is very kind and extremely patient.

Lady Diana Wills

CHAPTER ONE
the first lesson

Jimmy and Jenny had so much wanted to swim, and now the day of their first lesson had arrived. At the arranged time they went to the Swimming Baths to meet Mr. Wynne, who was to be their mentor in all matters of swimming.
(Fig.6.)

The swimming pool was large and noisy, with children shrieking and jumping in and out of the water. The noise was, from time to time, called to a sudden halt by a blast from the attendant's whistle, and the admonishing of some culprit for misbehaviour. All this was strange to Jimmy and Jenny, who up to now had been used to the solitude of their bath or to the fishpond in the garden.

As they walked down the steps at the shallow end, the whole area of the bath seemed to them as big as the ocean. As they stepped from the last step and stood on the pool floor the water reached just above their hips which enabled them to walk alongside the bath wall with ease.

(Fig.6.)

Jenny and Jim
meet Mr. Wynne

Exercise 1. Jumping up & down in the Water.

"Now" said Mr. Wynne, "I want you to jump up and down in the water, and try to let your shoulders go down under the water." (Fig. 7.)

Jimmy was able to cope with this one, but Jenny was a little timid because the water splashed up into her face. "All right", said Mr. Wynne. "Come with me, Jenny, and hold the rail of the bath. Now jump up and down — if it will help, hold your nose between your fingers". Jenny felt much happier this way, and, with Jimmy joining in, they both enjoyed the first exercise. Both felt very much more confident; as Mr. Wynne said, "As the body temperature gets accustomed to the water temperature, so we stop shivering and our teeth stop chattering".

Exercise 2. Holding the bar and pulling through the water.

"Now", said Mr. Wynne, "I want you to put on your inflatable arm bands. Having done this, to move back into the water until your arms are at full length, and then pull your body through the water towards the rail, keeping your legs stretched out perfectly straight". (Fig. 7(a))

Jimmy and Jenny thought this was great fun as they felt the water swirling past them with each pull of the arms. In no time they were able to lie on the surface of the water, and to pull and glide towards the rail.

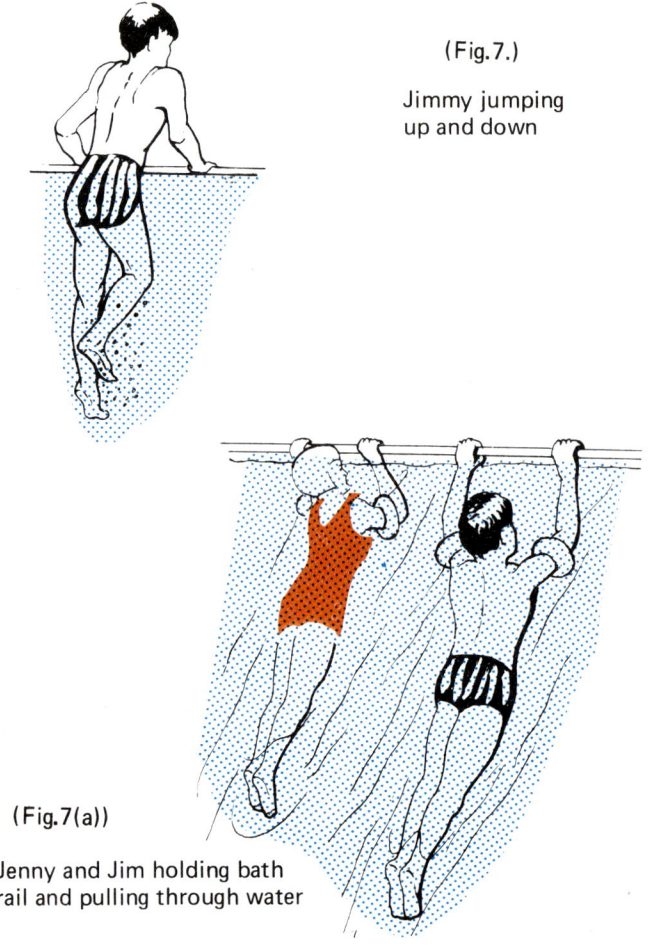

(Fig. 7.)
Jimmy jumping up and down

(Fig. 7(a))
Jenny and Jim holding bath rail and pulling through water

18

Exercise 3. Holding "float" and gliding to the rail.

"My last exercise this morning", said Mr. Wynne, "is gliding to the rail. For this, we must use something else to help you". He handed Jimmy and Jenny a foam float each, and showed them how to hold it with both hands. "Now, he said, "go into the water up to your armpits, put one foot in front of the other, straighten your arms on the surface of the water, hold the float at arms' length, and slightly bend the knee of the forward leg". (Fig.8.)

"I know", said Jenny. "It's the same as if you were starting to run in a race". "Exactly", said Mr. Wynne, "Now lie forward on the water, put your weight on your front foot, push from that foot keeping your arms, body and legs out straight, and glide forward towards the rail". Jimmy and Jenny found this a little difficult at first, chiefly because they held themselves too tensely, which caused them to throw their heads back or to drop their feet. Mr. Wynne, however, took each in turn, holding them on the surface with his left hand under the armpit and, holding their legs together and straight with his right hand, he gently launched them towards the bath rail. (Fig.9.)

This taught them the correct angle at which to lie on the surface, and gave them the feeling of buoyancy. Then Mr. Wynne returned to the first method of pushing from the front foot and gliding to the rail.

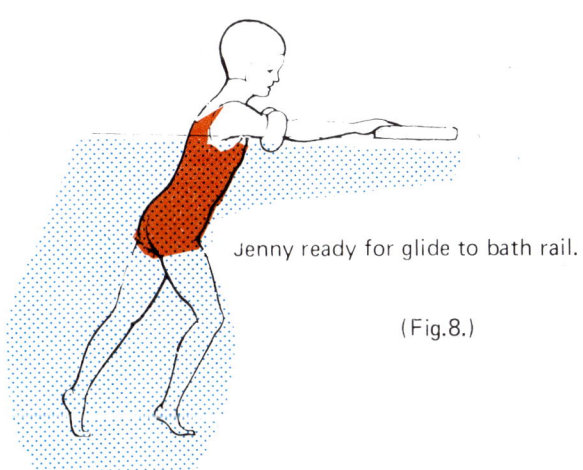

Jenny ready for glide to bath rail.

(Fig.8.)

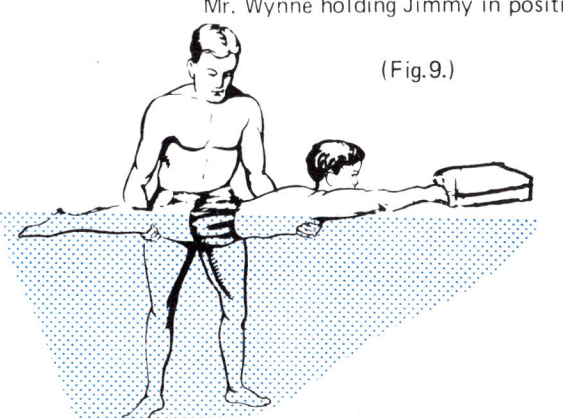

Mr. Wynne holding Jimmy in position

(Fig.9.)

19

Jenny was the first to be able to glide without assistance. With a cry of delight she shouted "I can do it", and proceeded to show that she could.

Jimmy, not to be outdone, strove hard, and at last he too could push and glide. Then, together, they competed as to who could be the first one to the rail. (Fig.10.)

CHAPTER TWO
front crawl

Exercise 1. Holding float and kicking legs

Jimmy and Jenny arrived brimful of confidence for their second lesson. Mr. Wynne gave them the floats and arm bands, and repeated the exercise of pushing and gliding to the rail. After a few more practises of the glide, he said "Right. I want you again to take up the position with your arms out straight, with one foot in front of the other, in the runner's attitude. Now push from the front foot, keep your arms straight, holding the float, and kick your legs".

Mr. Wynne stood behind them, and carefully watched the manner in which they kicked their legs. This would enable him to decide which stroke to teach them first; for, as he often said, "encourage children to do with their legs only that which comes naturally. Other strokes will follow at a later date". He watched carefully for some time, and then said "Very well, we are going to learn the front crawl". This he had finally determined upon when he noticed that they kept their legs fairly straight, and seemed to be able to thrash them up and down without a "spidery" action.

(Fig.10.)

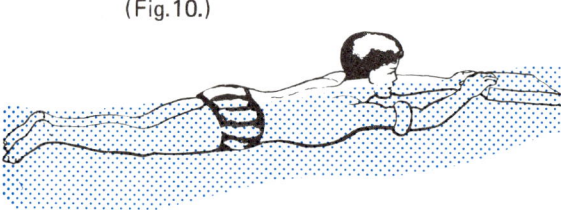

Jimmy gliding towards bath rail

the front crawl

Exercise 2. Holding float and doing leg action

Mr. Wynne now asked Jimmy and Jenny to stand a short distance from the rail, and to take up the previous position of crouching down in the water with one foot in front of the other, and the float held out at arms' length. "Now", he said, "lean forward into the water, allow your rear foot and leg to come up towards the surface, and push off from your front foot. As soon as you begin the glide, thrash your legs straight up and down".

Jimmy and Jenny tried this, but oh, what a performance. First they rolled one way, then the other, finally tipping over and letting go the float. "All this", Mr. Wynne explained, "is due to tension on one side or the other". So Jimmy and Jenny had to go over the exercise again and again. Each time they showed improvement and better balance; and, as the tension eased, confidence grew until both could lie forward, thrash their legs up and down and move to the rail on a level keel. (Fig.11.)

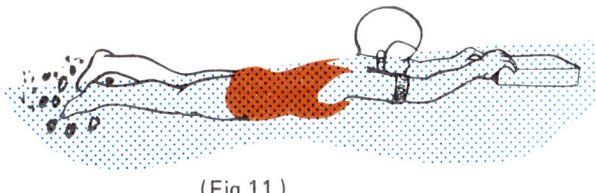

(Fig.11.)

Jenny and Jim gliding and kicking legs

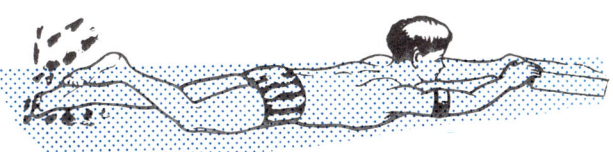

Exercise 3. Holding bath rail and doing leg action

"Now", said Mr. Wynne, "I want you to discard the foam floats, and to grasp the underside of the rail with both hands, fingers over and on the inside of the bar, thumbs outside. Press your elbows against the bath wall so that your legs come to the surface. Keep your legs together and straight, and turn your toes inward.

I want you now to thrash your legs up and down through the water, keeping your legs straight, but not stiff, and your ankles and knees very relaxed. Keep your elbows pressed against the bath wall as this will help to keep you on top of the water, kick up with the soles of your feet, don't kick too high or too deep." (Fig.12.)

At first Jimmy and Jenny found this fairly easy, but after a time their arms began to ache. Mr. Wynne told them to drop their legs and stand up for a moment, and then to repeat the leg action.

N.B. In Swimming Baths where there is no rail, then this exercise can be done by holding the lip of the surrounding water trough with fingers on top and elbows pressed against Bath wall.

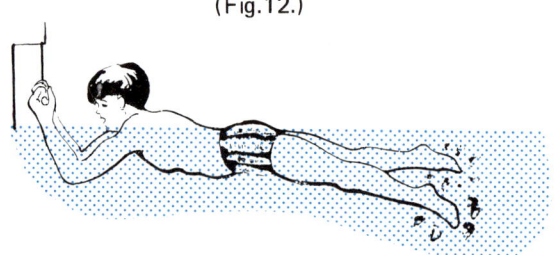

(Fig.12.)

Jimmy holding bath rail and thrashing his legs up and down

Exercise 4. Pushing from front foot into "Dog Paddle"

Mr. Wynne told Jimmy and Jenny to put on the inflatable arm bands and stand out in the water a few yards and face the bath rail.

"Place one foot in front of the other", he said, "and go down in the water until it reaches your armpits. Put your arms straight out in front of your head and lean your weight forward. Now push from your front foot, keep your legs fairly straight, kick them up and down, and at the same time reach forward with your hands, and pull them down through the water alternately". (Fig. 13 & 14)

Jenny seemed to manage this fairly well, but Jimmy would keep dropping his legs and doing a kind of hop Mr. Wynne insisted that he must keep kicking his legs up, up, up. After a time they were both able to lie forward on the water and, by doing the dog paddle, were able to swim to the side. (Fig. 14).

Next Mr. Wynne deflated each armband a little, and told Jenny and Jimmy to repeat the exercise of the "dog paddle". Then he asked them to remove one armband and repeat the exercise and, when their confidence had sufficiently increased, to remove the other. (Fig. 14a).

Eventually, by increasing the distance, Jimmy and Jenny found they could swim the width of the bath on the dog paddle.

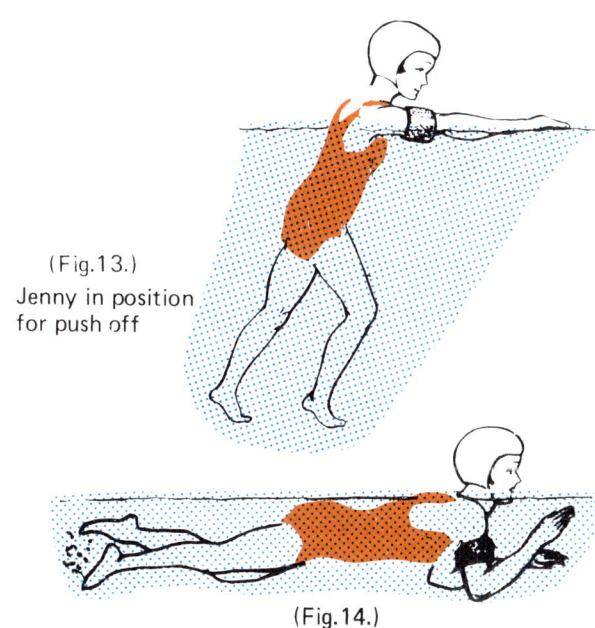

(Fig. 13.) Jenny in position for push off

(Fig. 14.)

Jenny and Jimmy doing dog paddle

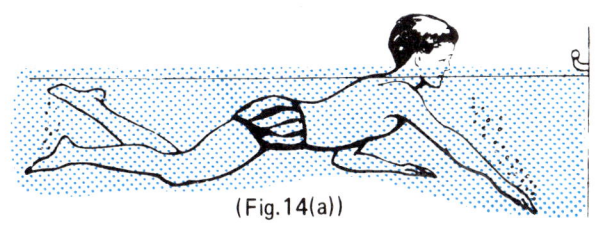

(Fig. 14(a))

Exercise 5. Arm lifting out of water

"When you return your arms after pulling them down through the water", said Mr. Wynne, "I want you to lift your shoulders as you make each alternate recovery stroke, so that your arms and elbows will automatically lift clear of the water. Then continue the arm movement out over the water and pull down through the water in a continuous rhythmic action". (Fig.15).

"Now, said Mr. Wynne, "I want you both to stand out in the water, facing the bath rail, with one foot in front of the other, arms straight out in front over the water. Push from your front foot and begin to pull down through the water. Then, as the elbow of the pulling arm begins to bend, lift that shoulder and bring your elbow and arm clear of the water, and continue this movement with both arms alternately".

Jimmy and Jenny found these movements a little complicated at first, and almost forgot to kick their legs; but, by practice over a short distance, they soon gained confidence and a regular rhythm. Gradually they extended the distance until they were able to swim the width of the bath on this stroke.

(Fig.15.)

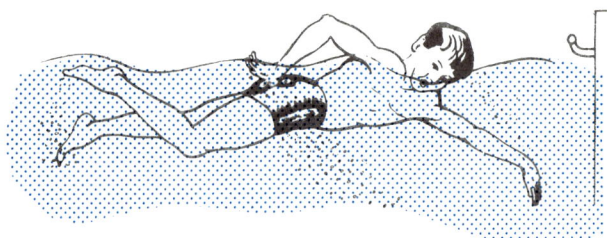

Jimmy lifting his shoulder and elbow on the recovery stroke

Exercise 6. Breathing

Experience had proved to Mr. Wynne that swimmers breathe naturally on one side or the other. Jimmy and Jenny were no exception to the rule. It was obvious to Mr. Wynne that Jimmy would snatch a breath on the left side, whilst Jenny turned more to the right. To Jimmy, therefore, he said, "As you lift your left shoulder and elbow out of the water, I want you to turn your head to the **left** and breathe '**IN**'. As your left arm goes out over and into the water I want you to turn your head to the **front** and breathe '**OUT**': continue to breathe in this way every time your left arm comes out of the water. (Fig.16.)

"You, Jenny, must do the same, **except** that in your case I want you to turn your head and breathe '**IN**' when your **right** arm is lifting, and '**OUT**' when your **right** arm is going forward and into the water". (Fig. 16.(a)).

At first Jimmy and Jenny could not get the correct timing in this exercise, but by practise over short distances they soon found that timing came quite naturally.

As a further help, Mr. Wynne asked them to do a little homework every day, by standing against and facing a wall, placing both hands against the wall, leaning their weight forward and turning their heads outward to breathe '**IN**' and turning to look at the wall to breathe '**OUT**'.

By doing this simple exercise for five minutes each day, they derived great benefit both in breathing correctly, and in improving their swimming stroke.

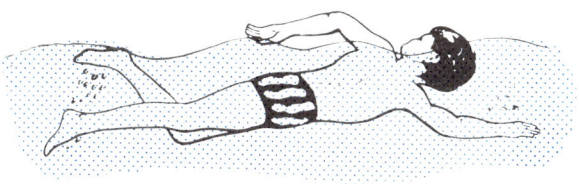

(Fig.16.)

Jenny and Jim front crawl breathing

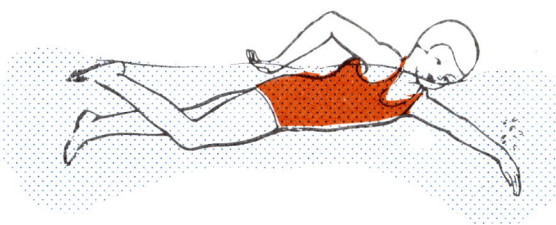

(Fig.16. (a))

25

Exercise 7. Breathing out into the water

Mr. Wynne asked Jimmy and Jenny to stand with their backs to the bath wall, and to reach behind and hold the rail with their fingers on the top, thumbs underneath, then to bend their knees and bring both feet up, pressing the soles of their feet against the wall, with the body leaning forward into the water. (Fig.17).

"Now", said Mr. Wynne, "keep your feet pressed against the wall, release your hands and put them straight out over the water. Put your face into the water, push hard from the wall with your feet and glide. As you are gliding, breathe out into the water". (Fig.18 & 19).

Exercise 8. Combining arm action with breathing

"Now", said Mr. Wynne, "I want you to push and glide in exactly the same way, but this time I want you, Jimmy to lift your left shoulder and arm as you come out of the glide, to turn your head to the left and breathe **'IN'**, allowing your head to lie sideways on the water, as it were

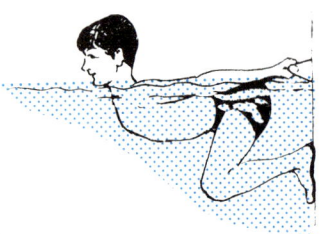

(Fig.17.)

Jimmy holding bath rail ready for push

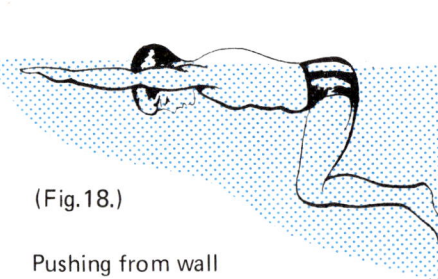

(Fig.18.)

Pushing from wall

(Fig.19.)

Gliding & breathing "Out" into water

on a pillow; then, as you extend your left arm out over and into the water, turn your head straight and breathe **'OUT'** into the water, and continue the strokes and breathing across the bath.

"I want you, Jenny, to do the same, but in your case you should breathe **'IN'** on the right hand side. As you come out of the glide, lift your right shoulder and arm, turn your head to the right and breathe **'IN'**. Then turn your head to the front and into the water to breathe **'OUT'**." (Fig.20).

Finally, do not over reach, as this will cause you to roll from side to side, and to assist breathing, glide forward a little more on the opposite shoulder to your breathing **'IN'** side.

For example:- if you breathe on the left, then glide forward a little more with your right arm and shoulder, and if on the right, then glide forward a little more on the left. This will also allow that extra second to breathe in, which is so important to prevent tiredness, (which of course is muscle tension)."

Jimmy and Jenny having arrived at a certain point of efficiency in the front crawl, Mr. Wynne felt that now was the time for them to proceed to the next step in the swimming world, and so we proceed to the Back Crawl.

(Fig.20.)

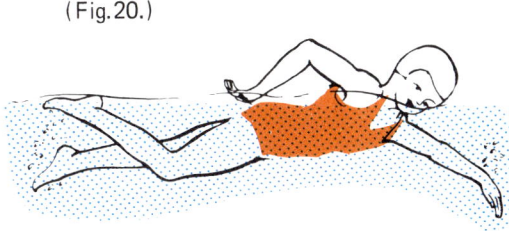

Jenny breathing in on front crawl

27

CHAPTER THREE
the back crawl

Mr. Wynne told Jimmy and Jenny that, in all probability, Jenny would be able to perform the back crawl more easily than Jimmy. He said that women, as a rule, do the back crawl quite naturally because of their bone structure and the natural relaxation of their muscles, which leads to easy breating and natural buoyancy. The legs of boys and men tend to sink, and effort on their part is needed to keep the legs to the surface.

Exercise 1

Mr. Wynne told them to hold the rail of the bath with both hands, and to place the soles of their feet against the wall of the bath, keeping their heels against the wall and hooking their toes under the rail. (Fig.21.)

"Now", said Mr. Wynne, "release both hands and lie gently back on the water, until you are lying out straight on the surface. Keep your hands by your side, look at the ceiling, and breathe naturally". (Fig.22.)

(Fig.21.)

Jimmy hooking toes under bath rail

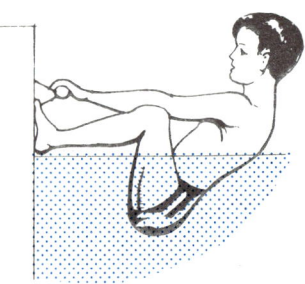

Jenny lying out on water

(Fig.22.)

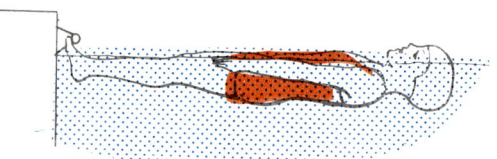

Jimmy found this rather difficult. He would release one hand before the other, which caused him to swing round to one side and lose his balance. Also, he held himself too tensely. Once he got used to releasing both his hands together, and lying out in a relaxed manner, he was able to do the exercise easily.

"Now", said Mr. Wynne, "drop your 'seats' in the water, lean forward to take hold of the rail, then drop your feet and stand up".

Exercise 2

"Lie out again on the water", said Mr. Wynne, "move your hands a short distance away from your sides, turn the palms of your hands inward, and move them back again to your sides with a slapping action, keep your wrists very relaxed. Now release your toes from the bath rail, keep your hands moving from and towards your thighs, and give a gentle push from the bath wall. Keep your legs out straight, but relaxed, float on the water and the continuous action of your hands pushing the water under your thighs and toward your feet will cause you to travel backward along the surface of the water". (Fig. 23.)

Jimmy and Jenny were able to do this fairly easily, Mr. Wynne told them that in future he would refer to this as the "sculling action".

Jenny lying out and doing "sculling action". (Fig. 23.)

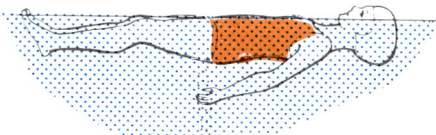

29

Exercise 3. The Flutter Kick

Jenny and Jimmy were now told to lie out in the water, as in the previous exercise, and to look up at the ceiling, to use their hands in the sculling action, and then to release their toes from the rail and kick their legs up and down. Jenny, as Mr. Wynne had predicted, was able to stay nicely on the surface and to do this with ease, but Jimmy's legs gradually sank, and eventually he was not moving at all. Mr. Wynne then said "Try to keep your knees under the water, flick your toes up through the water, breathe naturally, and do not forget to keep your hands moving from and to your side with wrists relaxed". (Fig. 24.)

Jimmy and Jenny repeated this exercise of the flutter kick again and again until both could scull across the bath with confidence, but each found difficulty in regaining their feet.

Exercise 4. Regaining Standing Position

To regain the standing position Mr. Wynne told Jimmy and Jenny to lean forward, to bring their knees up and tucked underneath their body in a crouching position or sitting position and now to lean forward as far as possible in a forward swimming position, then drop their legs and stand up, using the hands to scoop the water from back to front to assist the upright position. (Fig.25.)

After a few attempts both Jimmy and Jenny could manage this, particularly when they practised deliberately going from a back swimming position and into a breast stroke or front crawl stroke.

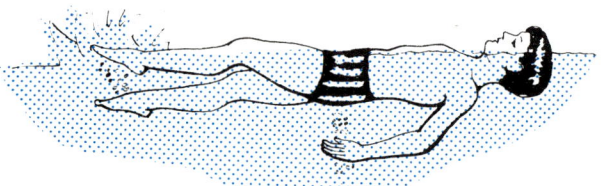

(Fig. 24.)

Jimmy doing the "Flutter" kick.

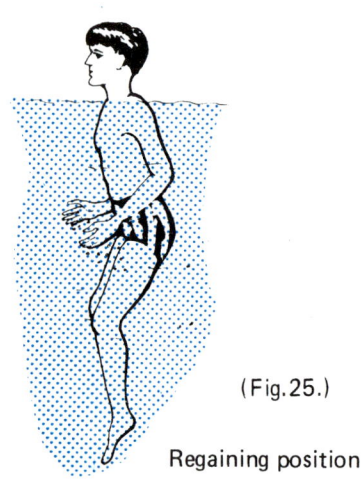

(Fig. 25.)

Regaining position

Exercise 5. Improving leg action with Float

"Now", said Mr. Wynne, "I want you to make use once more of the foam float, to lie out again on the water with your toes hooked on the bath rail. Hold the float with both hands, and keep it pressed against your chest. As soon as you feel comfortable, release your toes, keep the float pressed to your chest, and kick your legs up and down. The float will keep you on the surface, and kicking your legs will drive you through the water". (Fig.26.)

Jimmy and Jenny found this a great help, and were able to get across the bath with ease, particularly when they used their insteps when kicking up.

I realise that at some swimming baths there is no rail running around the bath side, so in that case we can find the foam float a great help. Hold the float as tightly as possible to your chest with both hands, then gently lie back on the water and kick your feet up and down. The chief action is the legs, so try and imagine you are kicking a ball out of the water, with the main action on your insteps and toes.

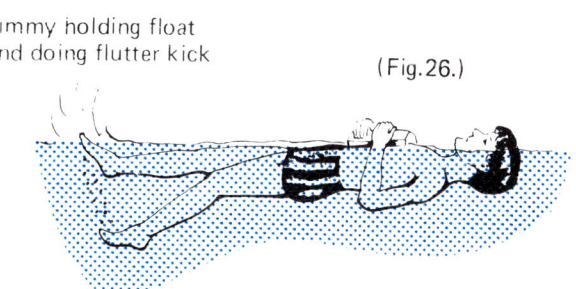

Jimmy holding float and doing flutter kick

(Fig.26.)

Exercise 6. Arm Action

Once more lying out on the water with their toes hooked on the bath rail, Jimmy and Jenny were told to place their hands by their sides.

"Use one arm only to begin with", said Mr. Wynne. "Move your right arm out of the water, and as you do so, turn the palm outward. Keep the arm straight, and continue the upward movement until your hand arrives at water level behind your head, allowing your little finger to enter the water first. Then, press your hand and arm outward and downward through the water and back to your side, turning the palm inward as you pull through the water, (in the way an oar is pulled when rowing.) Now do the same with the left arm. Repeat with the right arm. Now with the left arm". (Fig. 27).

"Now", said Mr. Wynne, "try using both arms alternately, in just the same way as you did with one arm. Start with the right arm, and as this arm begins the pull down through the water, begin to lift your left arm out of the water. Continue this arm action, first right, then left, turn your palm outward on the upward lift, and inward as you pull down through the water, each arm being rotated alternately".

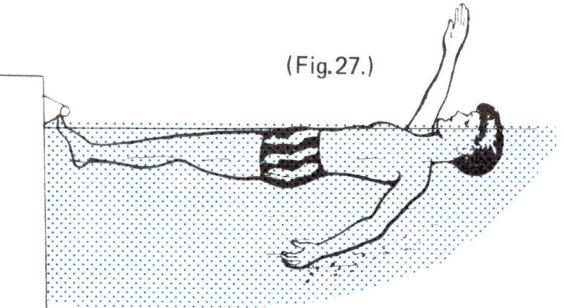

(Fig. 27.)

Jimmy with feet hooked under bath rail, practising back crawl

Exercise 7. Leg and Arm Movement

"Release your toes". said Mr. Wynne, "push from the wall with your feet, and kick them up and down in the flutter kick. At the same time, begin to lift your right arm forward and upward, and, as this arm starts the pull down through the water, lift the left arm and continue the rotating action with both arms". (Fig. 28).

Jenny did not find this action very difficult, but Jimmy, because he would bend his elbow instead of keeping it straight, found it hard going.

Mr. Wynne pointed out to them both, but more especially to Jimmy, that:

(1) They must keep their arms straight
(2) They must turn the palms of their hands outward as they lift their arms from the water
(3) They must flick their toes upwards through the water
(4) They must breathe naturally and easily
(5) When making the pull stroke, they must pull their hands and arms through the water in the way an oar is brought through the water in rowing
(6) They must ensure that their hands come right to their sides before starting the arm recovery. (Fig.29).
(7) That by turning the palms of their hands outward away from their face, it will prevent the water dripping from their hands into their face.

(Fig. 28.)

Jenny on right arm recovery stroke

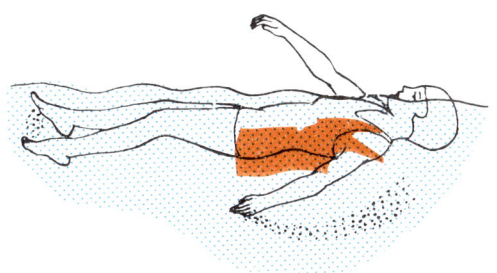

(Fig. 29.)

completing the left hand with arm to side on pulling stroke

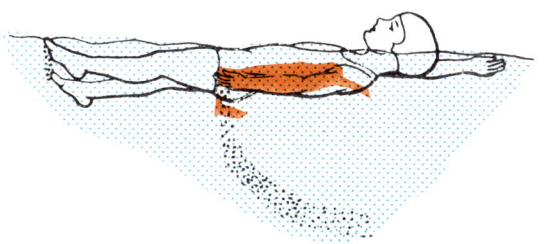

33

Girls, as Mr. Wynne pointed out, are naturally more relaxed and buoyant than boys, and Jenny soon began to look very professional in executing this stroke. However, with practise Jimmy soon found the correct balance of his body, which enabled him to do the back crawl quite comfortably and well. (Fig. 30).

Finally Mr. Wynne impressed on them both that to improve their stroke it was necessary to:

(1) Do plenty of "leg action" only, with and without the float.
(2) Try not to go too fast and so lose their rhythm.
(3) Keep breathing easily and naturally.
(4) Keep their arms straight, both in the recovery and the propelling action.
(5) Watch a line on the ceiling, in order to keep a straight course.
(6) Keep their bodies still, and avoid too much rolling from side to side.
(7) Try and ensure that your little finger enters the water first prior to the pull down through the water.

(Fig. 30.)

Jenny doing back crawl

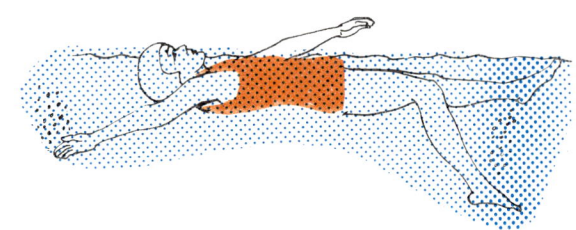

CHAPTER FOUR
the breast stroke

Some learners find this stroke easier to learn than the front crawl. "Also", said Mr. Wynne, "it is quite comfortable to use when swimming in the sea with waves coming at you". Jimmy and Jenny, therefore, must start again as beginners.

Exercise 1. Gliding to Rail

Jimmy and Jenny stood a few feet from, and facing, the bath rail. They then crouched down in the water, put their arms out straight on the surface, and again made use of the foam float, holding it at arms' length. (Fig. 31.)

"Now", said Mr. Wynne, "lean forward to the point at which you almost overbalance, then push from your front foot, keep your arms straight and glide to the rail with a kind of stretch action". They repeated this exercise until they were able to glide easily to the rail, with or without the float. (Fig. 31(a))

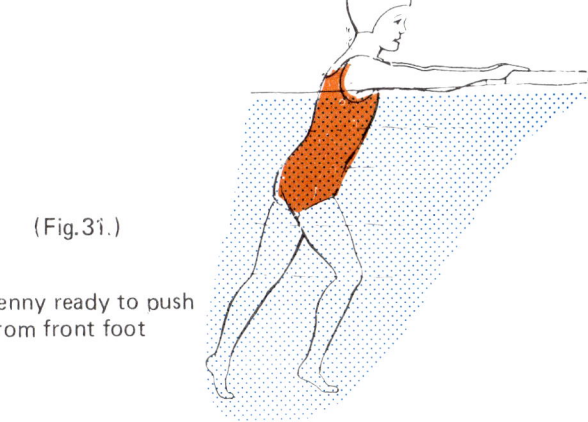

(Fig. 31.)

Jenny ready to push from front foot

and gliding to wall after push

(Fig. 31(a))

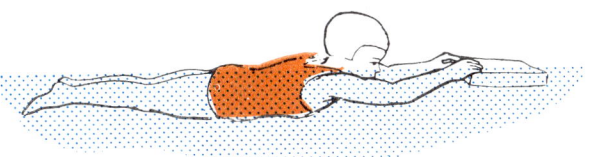

35

Exercise 2. Leg Action - holding bath rail to bring legs to surface

"Now", said Mr. Wynne, "hold the rail, fingers inside, with your elbows and forearms pressed against the bath wall. This will assist you to bring your legs up to the surface. Keep your legs together, and perfectly straight. (Fig. 32 (1)).

"Now, on the count of ONE, keep your legs straight, but press your heels together, slightly relaxing the knees. At TWO, bring your legs up, knees well bent and turn outwards, in a kind of diamond formation". (Fig. 32 (2)).

"At THREE, sweep the legs simultaneously outward, and kick backward". (Fig. 32 (3)).

"And, at FOUR, bring your legs together as in the starting position. Repeat this movement, and count to yourselves ONE, TWO, THREE and FOUR". (Fig. 32 (4)).

"Continue this exercise until you really have the leg action firmly in your minds". Here Mr. Wynne explained that they brought their legs up toward the body in order to be able to kick outward and backward in a circular movement, and that they kicked their legs backward in order to obtain a stronger drive through the water.

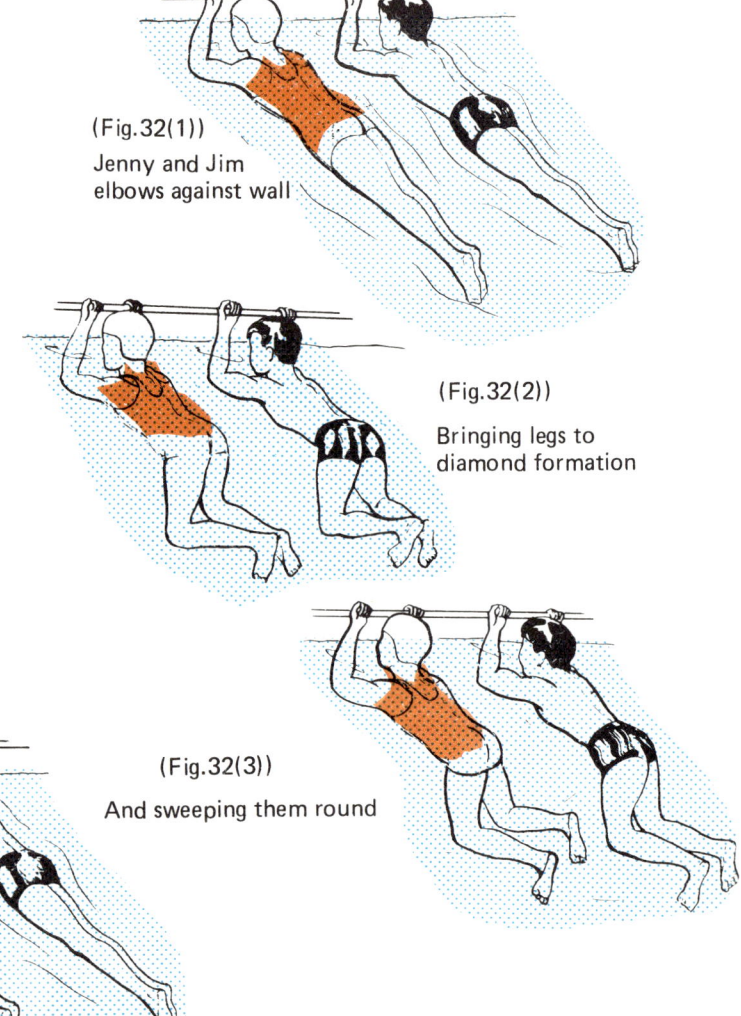

(Fig.32(1)) Jenny and Jim elbows against wall

(Fig.32(2)) Bringing legs to diamond formation

(Fig.32(3)) And sweeping them round

(Fig.32(4)) Completing leg action

Exercise 3. Leg Action with Float

"Once more", said Mr. Wynne, " stand out in the water a short distance from the rail, take your floats, hold them at arms' length, and crouch down in the water with one foot in front of the other". (Fig. 33).

"Lean forward, and push from your front foot, and then begin to bend your knees to a diamond formation ". (Fig. 34).

"Then swish your legs out and around, and back together again. (Fig. 35).

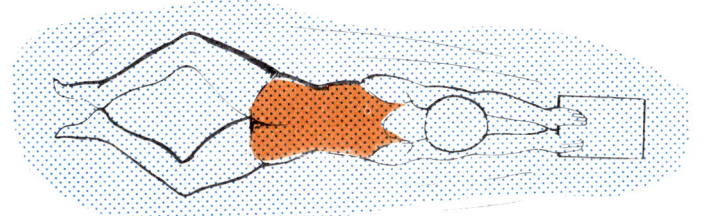

(Fig. 33.) Jenny holding float ready for push from front foot

(Fig. 34.) Bending legs to diamond formation

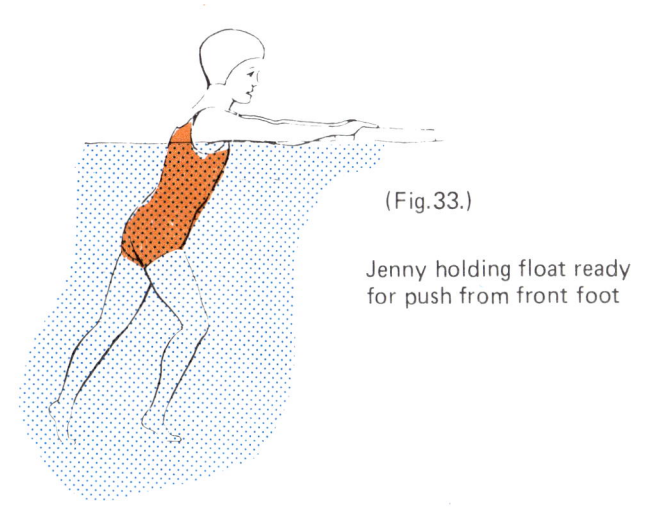

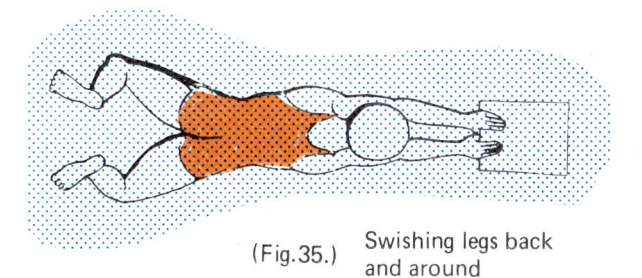

(Fig. 35.) Swishing legs back and around

Exercise 4. Glide to rail with Leg Action

"Now discard the float", said Mr. Wynne, "and stand about three paces from, and facing, the bath rail. Crouch down in the water and place one foot a little in front of the other, with your arms straight out on the surface. Now lean forward, put your weight on the front foot and push off from this foot". (Fig. 36).

"Keep your arms and legs together, and straight, and glide toward the bath rail". (Fig. 36 (a)).

"At the end of the glide, take hold of the bath rail with both hands, and at the same time bring your legs up, knees turned outward in a diamond formation". (Fig. 36 (b))

"Sweep your legs outward and backward in a circular movement". (Fig. 36 (c)).

"Bring your legs together again, and straight". (Fig. 36 (d)).

Jimmy and Jenny found this a little difficult at first, because they did not lie sufficiently forward in the water, and because they were in too much of a hurry to grab at the rail. Their troubles vanished as soon as they had learnt to lean well into the water, and to glide all the way to the rail.
In the case of no bath rail, hold the lip of water channel.

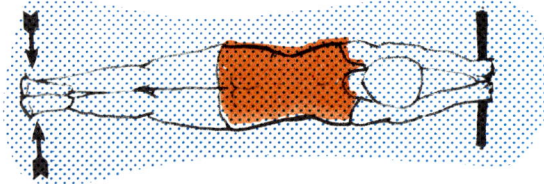

Legs together and straight
(Fig.36.(d))

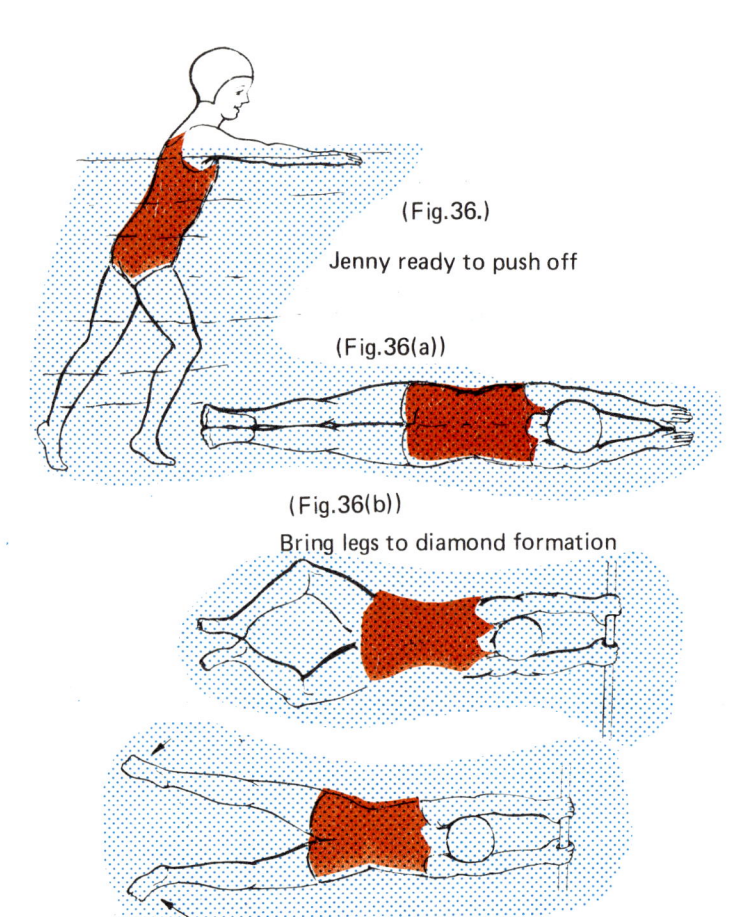

(Fig.36.)
Jenny ready to push off

(Fig.36(a))

(Fig.36(b))
Bring legs to diamond formation

Swishing legs round
(Fig.36(c))

Exercise 5. Arm and Leg Action

"Now", said Mr. Wynne, "take the same stance, lean forward and push from your front foot, arms straight out in front". (Fig. 37 (a)).

"Then sweep your arms out and around, hands cupped and turned slightly outward, and bring them to a point in line with, but a little in front of, your shoulders". (Fig. 37 (b)).

"Begin bending your knees, heels touching, bringing the legs up into a diamond formation, and your hands and arms to a point just in front of the chin". (Fig. 37 (c)).

"Stretch your arms forward, and at the same time, swirl your legs outward and backward in a circular movement". (Fig. 37 (d)).

"Bring your legs together, lying out straight on the water". (Fig. 37 (e)).

This exercise seemed complicated to Jimmy and Jenny, but by practising first one complete stroke, then two, and then three consecutive strokes, they were soon able to swim confidently across the bath. Always remembering to make the arm movement first, and to bring the knees and heels up as the arms came around, then as the arms go forward to swish the legs out and around and together, or in other words imagine you have to make your legs drive your arms forward.

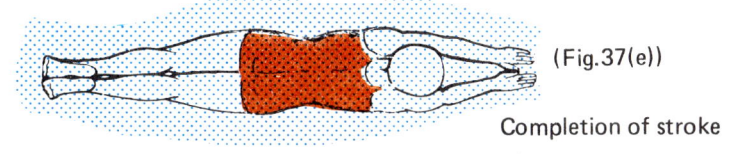

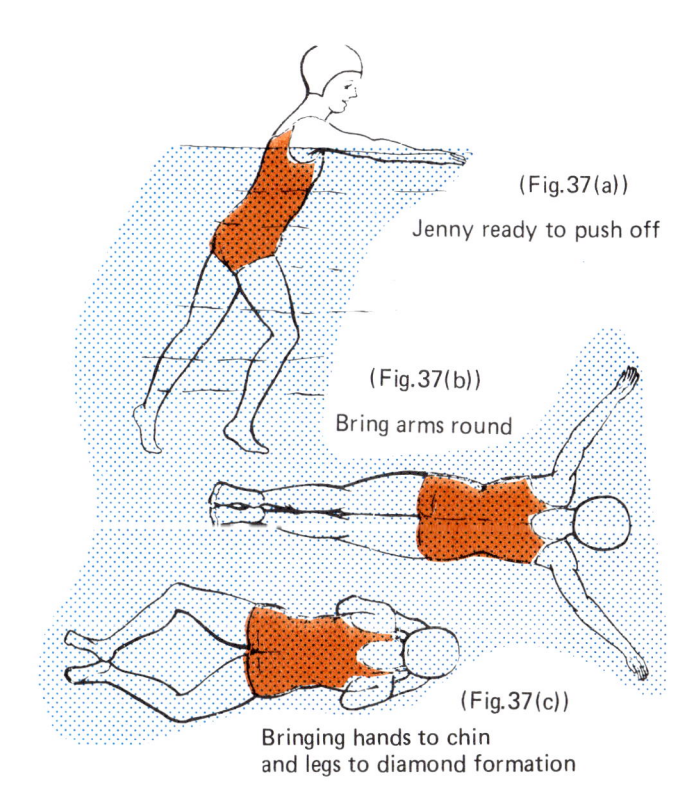

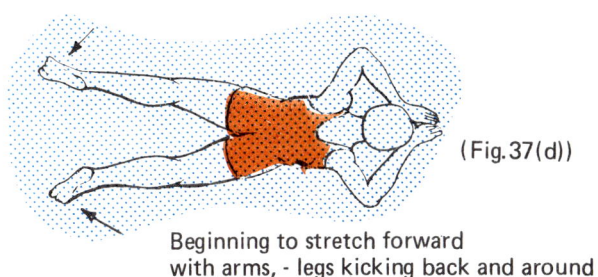

(Fig. 37(a)) Jenny ready to push off

(Fig. 37(b)) Bring arms round

(Fig. 37(c)) Bringing hands to chin and legs to diamond formation

(Fig. 37(d)) Beginning to stretch forward with arms, - legs kicking back and around

(Fig. 37(e)) Completion of stroke

Exercise 6. Breathing

"Breathing", said Mr. Wynne, "is most important. As soon as you thrust your hands and arms forward, breathe 'OUT'. As your arms are swept out and round to the position almost in line with your shoulder, breathe 'IN'. The principle to follow is - arms forward, breathe 'OUT'; arms sweeping round, breathe 'IN'. Then breathe 'OUT' and 'IN' with every stroke". (Fig. 38 (a) and (b)).

With practice, Jimmy and Jenny were able to synchronise their leg and arm movements with their breathing and to glide and swim the breast stroke with ease. They timed their breathing wrongly occasionally, which caused them to splutter; but, by continuing the stroke and spitting the water out, they quickly regained the rhythm.

Mr. Wynne insisted that they must keep their hands under the water, particularly when sweeping them round. They should press down a little on the sweep round, as this would give more pressure on the water, and would automatically cause their faces to lift, and assist the breathing 'IN'. Also, it would add more power to the pull stroke of the arms and prevent splashing.

To assist in the correct way to breathe, hold the float out at arms length (as shown in Fig.33.), and each time the legs are "swished" around (as in Fig.34.) then breathe 'OUT' and when bending the legs up to the diamond formation breathe 'IN'. From this simple exercise much benefit will be derived in co-ordinating the stroke and breathing.

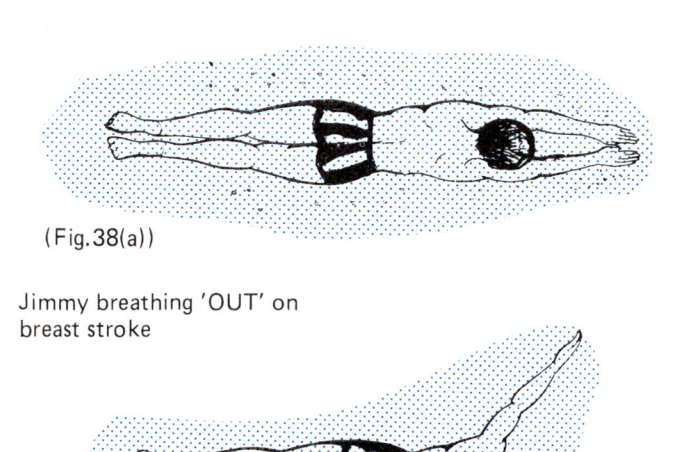

(Fig.38(a))

Jimmy breathing 'OUT' on breast stroke

(Fig.38(b))

Breathing 'IN', arms coming round

CHAPTER FIVE
the back stroke or life saving stroke

Mr. Wynne said to Jimmy and Jenny "This is a stroke everyone should learn. It is called, quite rightly, the Life Saving Back Stroke. If you know which stroke to use in order to save a life, this surely can be regarded as a very desirable achievement. So mark, learn and remember the motto of the Royal Life Saving Society: 'Whomsoever you see in distress, recognise in him a fellow man'".

Exercise 1. Lying out on the water

"So now", said Mr. Wynne, "take hold of the bath rail with both hands, place your heels against the bath wall, and grip the bath rail with your toes. Now release both hands simultaneously, and gently lie back on the water. Hands by your sides, palms inward, look at the ceiling and breathe naturally and easily, in the same way as you did for the back crawl. (Fig. 39.)

(Fig. 39.)

Jenny lying out on water

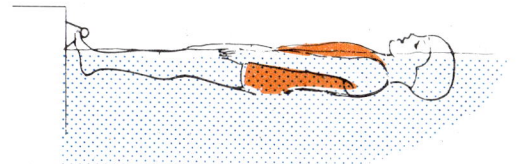

Exercise 2. Sculling Movement

"Release your toes, use your hands in a flipping or fin action, away and towards your thighs (in the same way as you smack your sides in cold weather in order to get warm), and glide along the surface of the water in the sculling movement. Remain relaxed, and breathe naturally". This exercise, of course, was now easy for them both. (Fig. 40).

Exercise 3. Leg Action

"Now", said Mr. Wynne, 'once more take up the position with your toes hooked on the rail, and lie out on the water as described in Exercise 1. Release your toes, and begin to glide from the rail, keeping the upper part of your legs in line with your body; bend your knees, and allow the lower part of your legs to drop down. Continue the leg action with your knees opening sideways, swirling your feet and legs outward and around in a circular movement, and bring them together again in line with your body. Keep the knees just under the surface, which will prevent the wash from the leg movement splashing your face. Make the circular movement of your legs in a fairly wide sweep, strong but not jerky, propelling the body with your legs, at the same time sculling with the hands". (Figs. 41 (a) and (b)).

(Fig. 40.)
Jenny sculling along the surface of the water

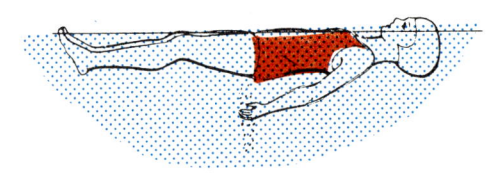

(Fig. 41(a))
Dropping her legs

(Fig. 41(b))
Swishing legs around

Exercise 4. Leg Action with Float

"Once more", said Mr. Wynne, "hold the float with both hands close to your chest. Lie out flat on the water, and practise the leg kick by bending your knees and sweeping your legs out and around. Breathe normally and easily, and look at the ceiling". (Fig 42 (a) and (b)).

Exercise 5. Complete Leg Action

"Now dispose of the float", said Mr. Wynne, "place your hands on your thighs - or, if preferred, fold them on your chest, and use your legs only. A good leg movement is essential, because in life-saving the legs have to do the whole work. This enables your hands to be free to hold your distressed subject, and to tow him or her through the water". (Flg. 43).

Mr. Wynne reiterated that they must not hold their breath. They should breathe in and out naturally, and if a little water should splash in the face, they should hold their breath for a moment, and then revert to normal breathing.

How to carry out rescue and resuscitation are described in Appendices "A" and "B".

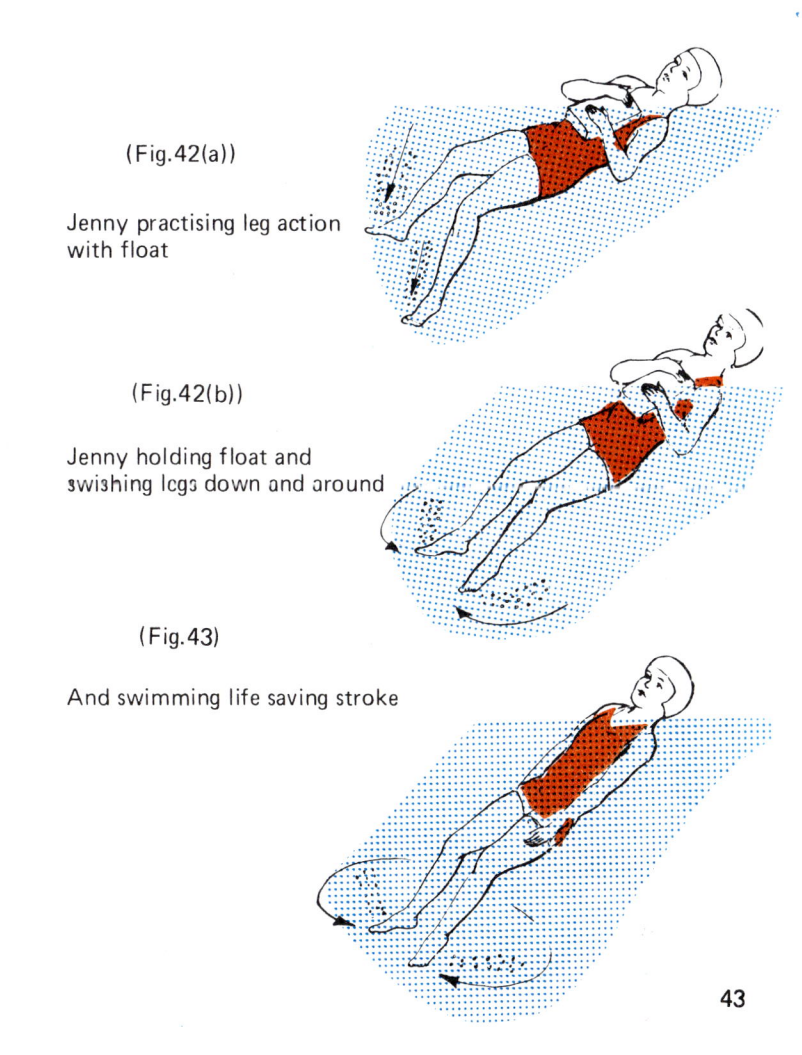

(Fig.42(a))

Jenny practising leg action with float

(Fig.42(b))

Jenny holding float and swishing legs down and around

(Fig.43)

And swimming life saving stroke

CHAPTER SIX

jumping into the water and treading water

Exercise 1. Jumping from bath edge towards Instructor

"First", said Mr. Wynne, "I want you to stand at the edge of the bath with your toes just over the edge, so as to prevent you from slipping. Then slightly bend your knees. and place your arms by your sides. Now jump in to me". (Fig.44.)

Mr. Wynne held up his hands, and first Jimmy jumped, then Jenny, both being caught by Mr. Wynne. (Fig.44(a))

(Fig.44.)

Jenny ready to jump

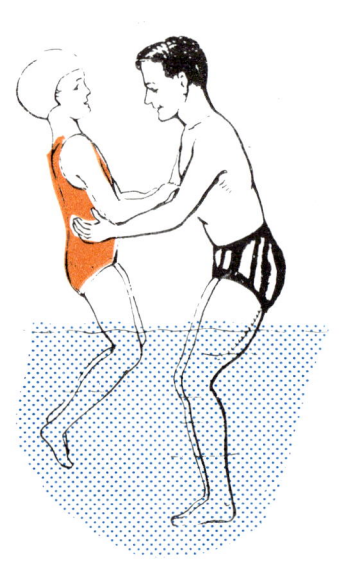

(Fig.44(a))

Jenny jumping to Mr. Wynne

44

Exercise 2. Jumping into water unaided

Mr. Wynne gradually lowered his hands and encouraged them to jump until both could jump in unaided. Then he gradually worked down the bath toward the deep end, encouraging them both to jump and swim back to the side.

Jimmy and Jenny found that, by holding their breath when jumping into deep water, and remaining calm, they quickly came to the surface. By lying forwards, they were able to swim to the side. (Fig.45. and 45(a))

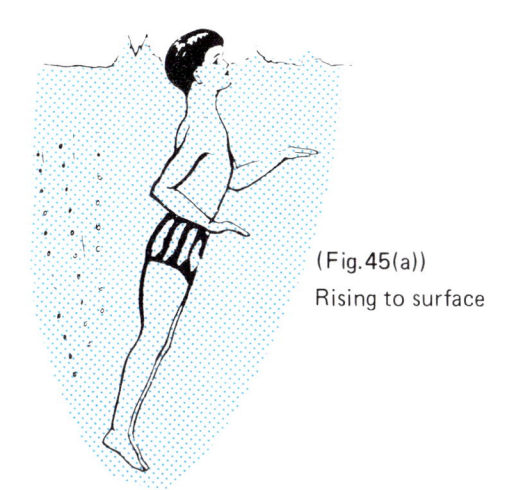

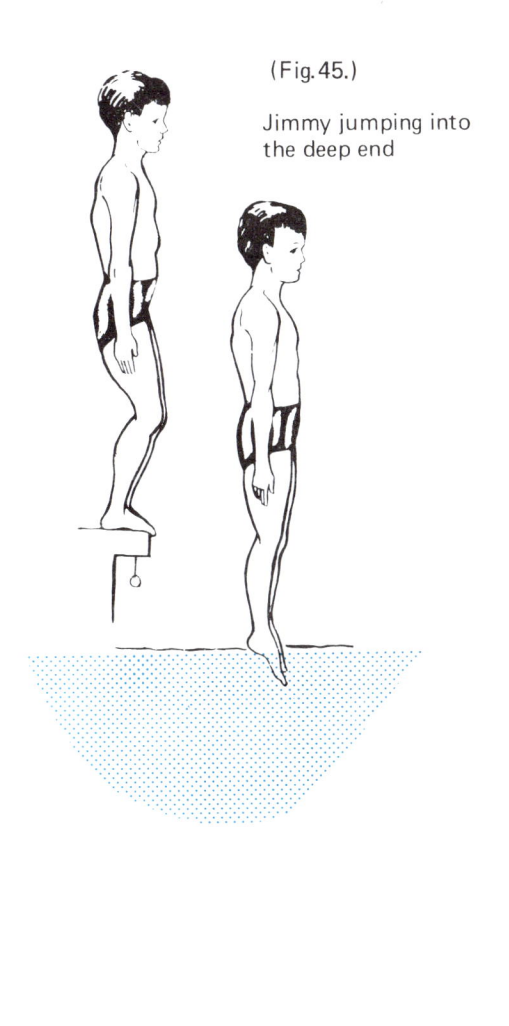

(Fig. 45.)

Jimmy jumping into the deep end

(Fig. 45(a))

Rising to surface

TREADING WATER

"Now" said Mr. Wynne, "I also want to teach you how to remain on the water by what is known as "Treading Water" and as the word implies, so that is what it is.

"After jumping into deep water or if you get stopped in 'mid-stream', by someone swimming across in front of you, just remain upright in the water, tread the water with your feet and press your hands down on the water in a kind of hand press movement.

"The best way in which I can describe the leg movement is a breast stroke action with the legs, standing upright in the water, instead of lying forward. In other words, you bend your knees up and 'swish' your legs around and at the same time press down with your hands. Get a kind of 'bouncing' action up and down in the water — 'bouncing' upward with each 'swish' of your legs". (Fig.46.)

After a little practice, Jenny and Jimmy became quite proficient, and derived much confidence in the knowledge of being able to remain stationary in the water without becoming frustrated when faced with a little difficulty or prevented from swimming to the side of the bath.

If difficulty is experienced in bending and sweeping the legs around then another way is by using the legs as if climbing up stairs in an up and down movement, but use the hands the same.

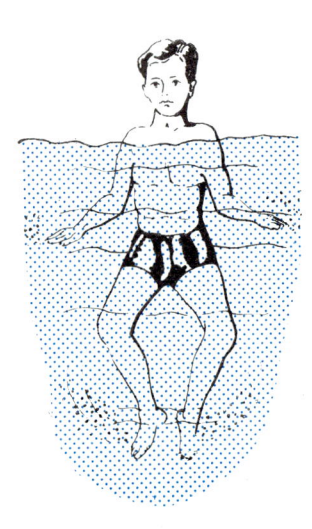

(Fig.46.))
Jimmy treading water

CHAPTER SEVEN
diving

Many people, even after learning to swim feel scared of diving, but there is nothing to fear provided a few simple rules are followed, and so together with Jenny and Jim who, having become used to jumping into the water and getting their heads under, knew there was really nothing to fear, let us begin with Exercise 1.

Exercise 1. Holding rail to push and Glide downward.

Mr. Wynne placed Jimmy & Jenny in the water near the shallow end, with their backs to the wall. "Now" he said, "grip the bath rail, keep your fingers on top of the rail, and your thumbs underneath. Place the soles of your feet against the wall, straighten your arms and lean your body forward into the water." (Fig.47(a))

"Now put your head in the water and hold your breath. At the same time release your grip of the rail, stretch your arms straight out in front of your head, and push from the wall with your feet. Glide downward towards the bottom of the bath, then turn your hands upward towards the surface. This will assist you to rise easily and smoothly through the water to the surface." (Fig.47(b))

After practise, Jimmy and Jenny found this exercise very enjoyable, and not half so frightening as they had imagined.

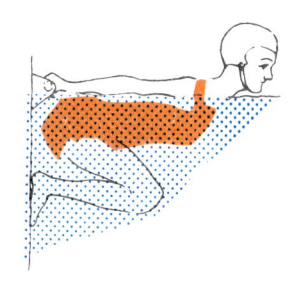

(Fig.47(a))

Jenny ready for push from wall

(Fig.47(b))

Jenny gliding downward after push from the wall

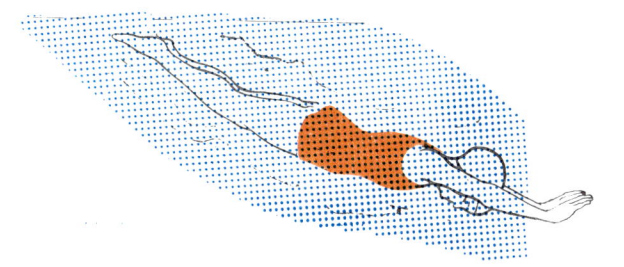

Exercise 2. Diving from bath steps

"Now", said Mr. Wynne, "I want you to stand on the top or on the second of the steps leading into the bath. Place your arms straight out in front, keep your head well down below the level of your arms, and lean forward. Just as you feel you are about to overbalance, push from the steps with your feet, and dive forward and downward into the water". (Fig.48.)

Jimmy and Jenny gave themselves a bit of a smack to their tummies as they met the water. This, Mr. Wynne said, was because they threw their heads **back** instead of keeping them **down** until they were under the water. More practice was necessary before they acquired the confidence to go forward and down.

After this exercise Mr. Wynne took them to where the water was deep enough to come up to their shoulders when they stood on the bottom of the bath.

"We are now", he said, "going to learn the Seal Dive".

(Fig.48.)

Jimmy diving from bath steps

Although children like Jimmy and Jenny enjoy this exercise, I doubt if adults would care to try it and suggest they go straight from Exercise 2 to Exercise 4.

As shown in (Fig.50.)(Page 50)

Exercise 3. The Seal Dive

"Lie out on your tummies", said Mr. Wynne, "with your head and shoulders over the edge of the bath, and your legs out straight. Take hold of the bath rail, and gradually pull yourselves forward until you overbalance into the water. Then put your arms out straight, as soon as you feel yourselves overbalancing, slide forward and down into the water" (Fig.49.)

Jimmy and Jenny thought this really super and continued until they were able to slide into the water and glide easily toward the bottom of the bath.

(Fig.49.)

Jenny doing the seal dive

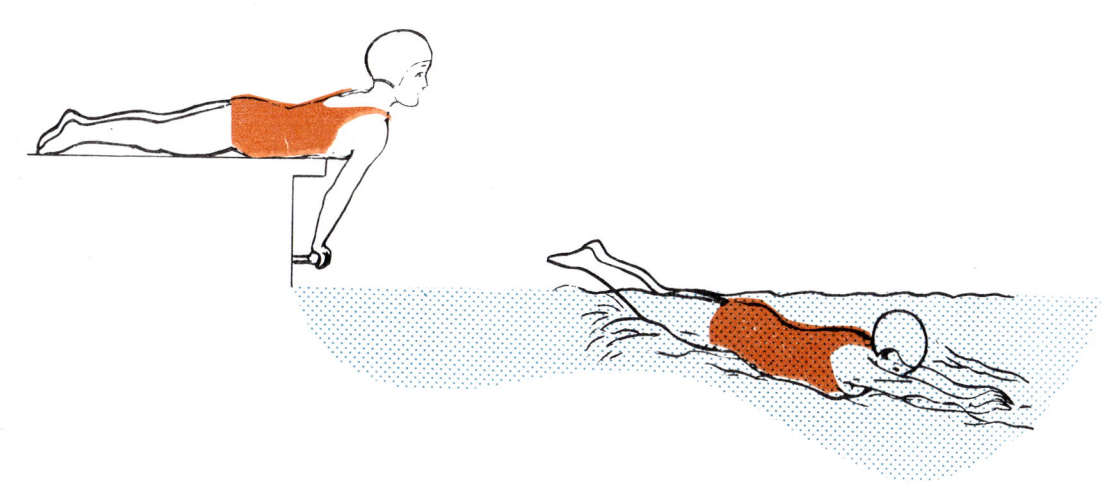

Exercise 4. Diving from one knee

Mr. Wynne took Jimmy and Jenny a little further along the side of the bath, and said "Now I want you to kneel on one knee and place your other foot on the edge of the bath wall, with your toes overlapping the edge. Place your arms straight forward with your head between your arms". (Fig.50.)

"Gradually lean forward, putting your weight on your front foot, keep your weight going forward all the time, and as you are on the point of overbalancing, straighten your leg. Keep your head **down**, and dive forward and **down** into the water".

Again Jimmy and Jenny found this difficult at first because they threw their **heads back** instead of keeping them **down**. This caused them to "belly flop". However, with practice they overcame this, and were able to go forward and to enter the water smoothly and cleanly. (Fig.51.)

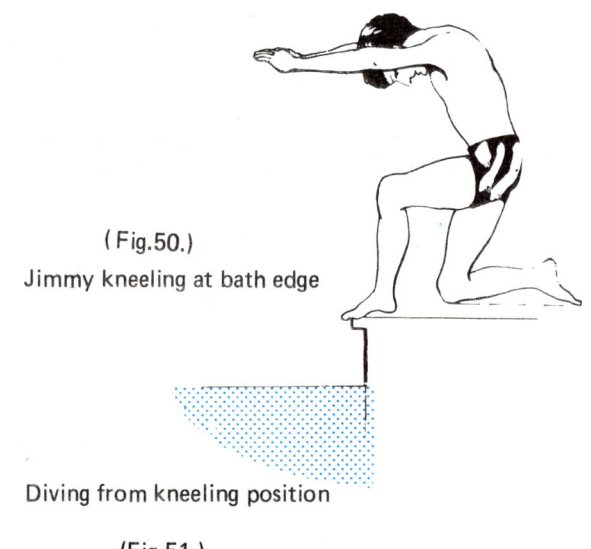

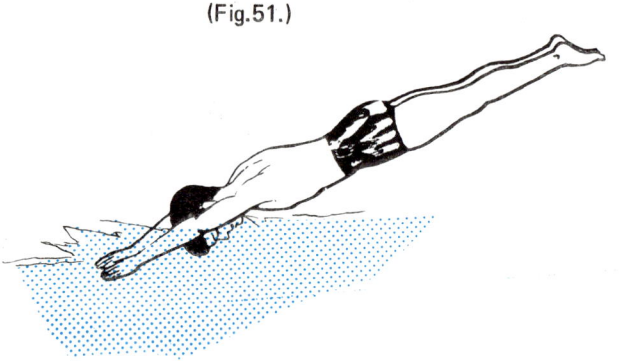

(Fig.50.)
Jimmy kneeling at bath edge

Diving from kneeling position

(Fig.51.)

Exercise 5. Diving from front foot

"Stand once more on the edge of the bath", said Mr. Wynne, "place one foot in front of the other, with the toes overlapping the edge, with the other foot about eighteen inches behind. Put your hands straight above your head, arms pressing against your ears, relax, and slightly bend your front leg and knee". (Fig.52(a))

"Now lean your body forward, gradually putting your weight on the front foot. Continue to go forward, allowing your rear foot to lift naturally from the floor. Then, just as you are on the point of overbalancing, lean forward and push from your front foot. Do not forget to **keep your head down** below the level of your arms". (Fig.52(b))

"Do not panic", said Mr. Wynne, "or be in a hurry to surface. Simply keep your head down and your body and limbs in a perfectly straight line, and allow your whole body to go down through the water; hold your breath, turn your hands up, and you will quickly rise to the surface. Then, just lie forward and swim". (Fig.52(c))

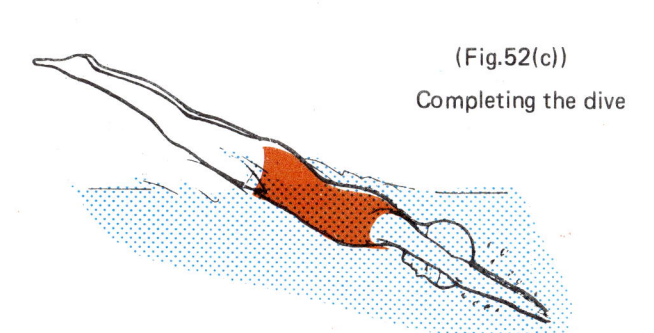

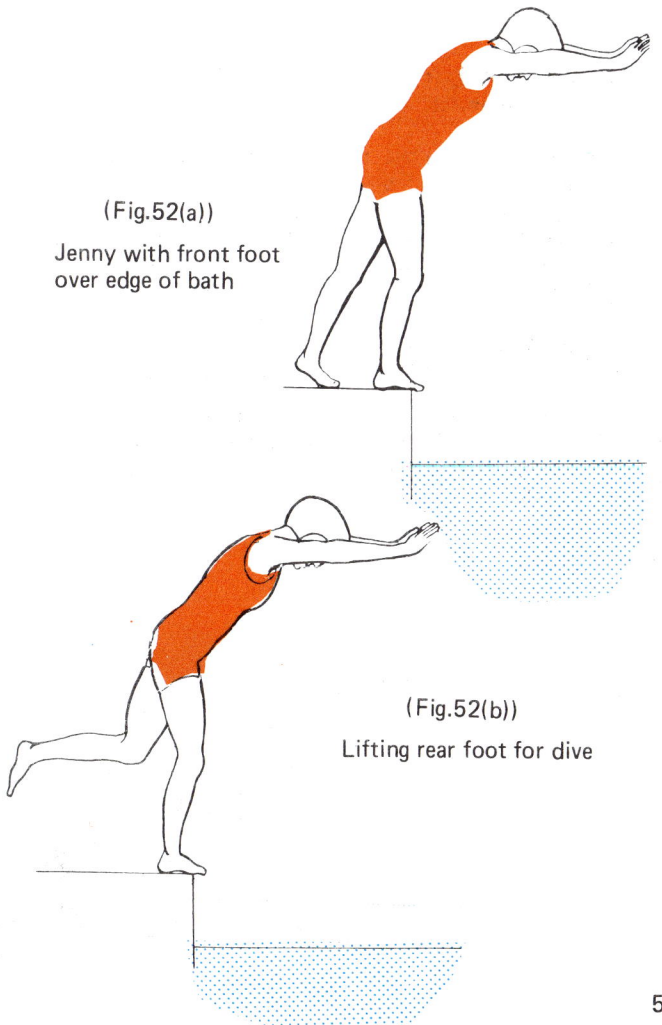

(Fig.52(a))
Jenny with front foot over edge of bath

(Fig.52(b))
Lifting rear foot for dive

(Fig.52(c))
Completing the dive

Exercise 6. Diving from edge with both feet together

Stand on the edge of the bath, with toes over and gripping the edge. Relax the knees and touch your toes with the tips of your fingers. Keep your knees bent in that position and raise your arms to a position in line with your shoulders. Lean forward and at the point of overbalancing, hold your breath and roll forward and downward into the water. Keep arms and body out straight, turn your fingers upward and so glide to the surface. But if necessary swim up through the water to the surface. (Fig.53(a), 53(b))

Note:— By continuous practise one can soon dive from an upright stance (English header) but as I said at the commencement, this book is for beginners and practise makes perfect.

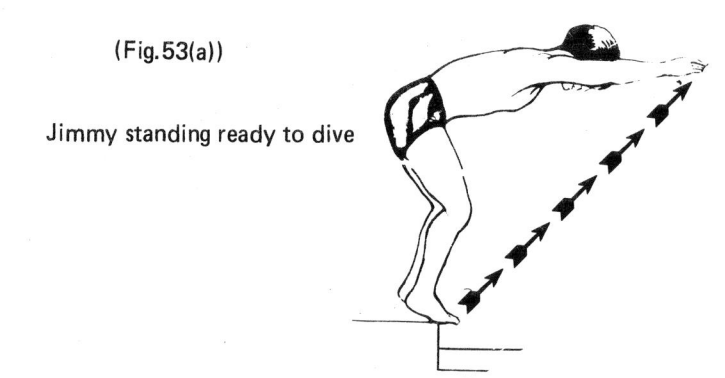

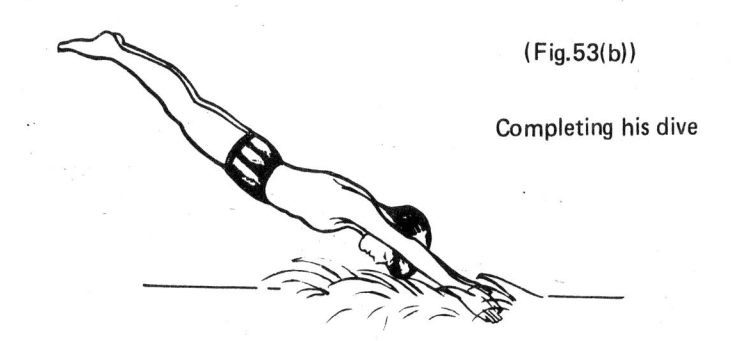

(Fig.53(a))

Jimmy standing ready to dive

(Fig.53(b))

Completing his dive

Exercise 7. The Racing Dive

"Finally", said Mr. Wynne, "I want to teach you the elementary principles of the Racing Dive". Again Jimmy and Jenny took up their positions on the side of the bath, with their toes overlapping the edge.

"Now", said Mr. Wynne, "stand with your feet 'hip width' apart, with your hands by your side but slightly behind the hips. Relax both knees, and lean your body forward, head down". (Fig.54(a))

"Put all your weight on both feet, relax both knees, spring from your feet, and hurl yourself well out into the water. At the same time, swing your arms forward and stretch them out in front of you. Do not forget it is **most essential** to keep your head down". (Fig.54(b))

"After entering the water, continue to glide to the surface, and then begin your leg and arm actions to swim straight on across the bath". (Fig.54(c))

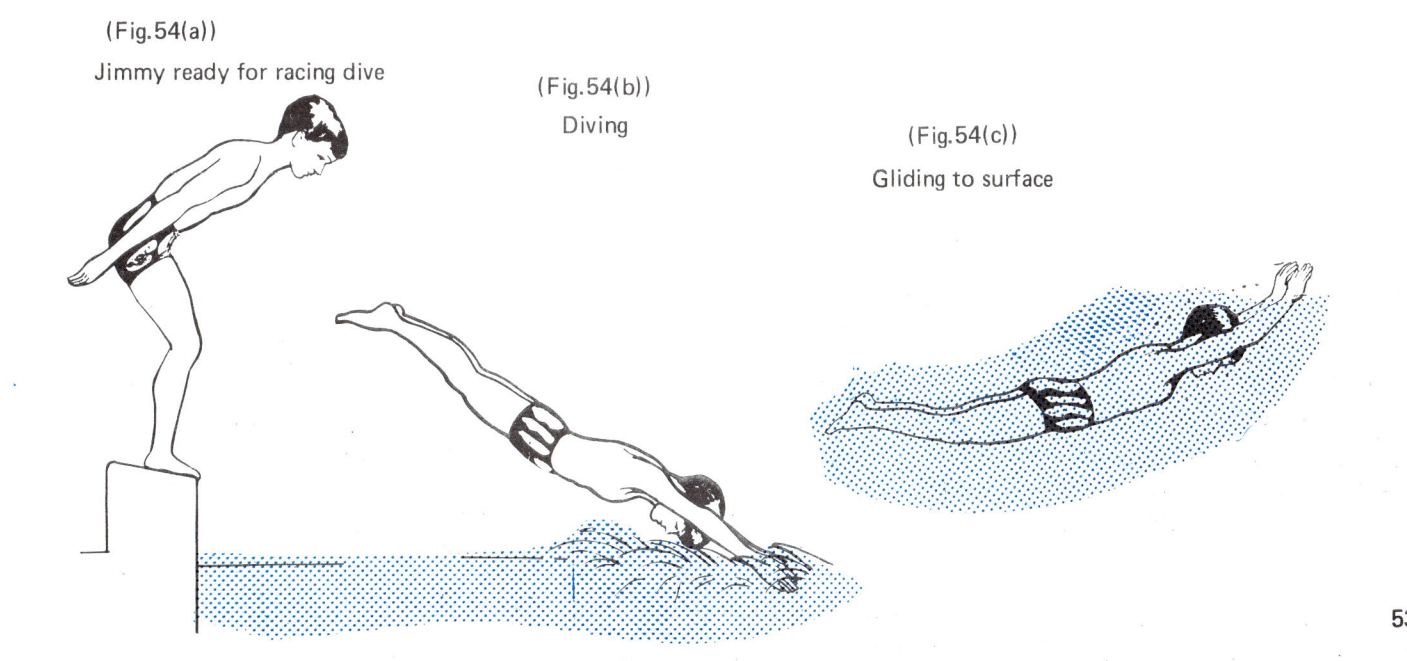

(Fig.54(a))

Jimmy ready for racing dive

(Fig.54(b))

Diving

(Fig.54(c))

Gliding to surface

Exercise 8. Diving to recover object

As an added interest, and in order to assist Jimmy and Jenny to enter the water with head down and at the correct angle, Mr. Wynne placed a small weighted diving block on the bottom of the bath, in the deep end, about two yards from the edge. He told them to take up the diving stance on the edge of the bath, to look at the block of wood, and then to dive straight down to it and, if possible, to pick it up with both hands and return with it to the surface. (Figs. 55(a), 55(b), 55(c), 55(d))

Jimmy overshot the wooden block, and Jenny could not quite make the depth. However, after a few practises, they both learned to enter the water correctly. By keeping both arms stretched forward in front of their heads, and opening their eyes under the water, they were able to dive right on to the block and recover it.

(Fig.55(a))
Jimmy ready to dive for block

(Fig.55(b))
Picking up block

(Fig.55(c))
Pushing off from bottom

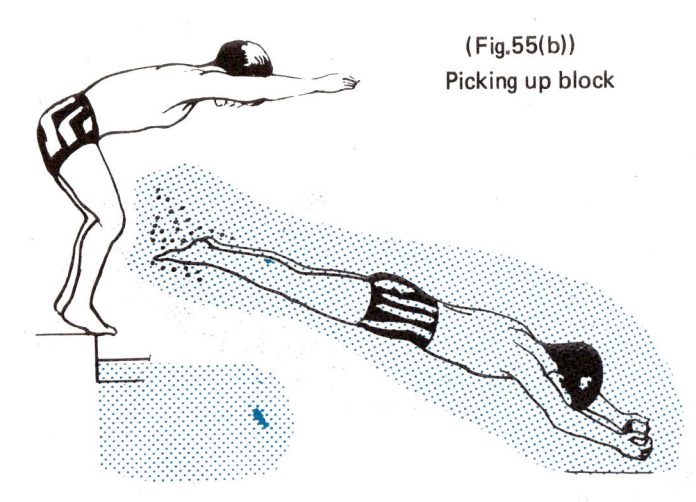

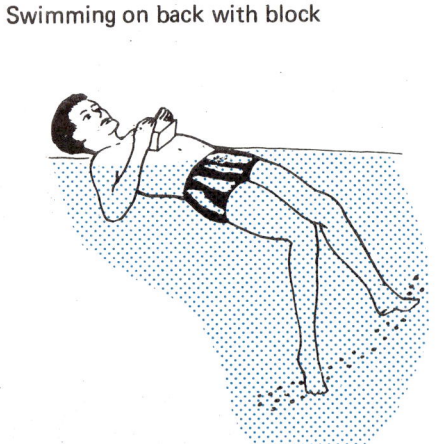

(Fig.55(d))
Swimming on back with block

Exercise 9. The Surface Dive

This dive is better known as the "Duck Dive", because in performing it, one descends head first from a swimming position, down through the water in order to recover an object below the surface, in exactly the same way as a duck dives down head-first in search of food.

Mr. Wynne dropped the wooden diving block into about 3 ft. of water. "I want you", he said, "to swim along the surface, and to look down at the block as you are swimming towards it. When you are a short distance from it, thrust your head and arms deep into the water and throw your legs up straight, and then pull with your hands through the water". (Fig.56(a))

"Straighten your arms out again, look at the block, and pick it up". (Fig.56(b))

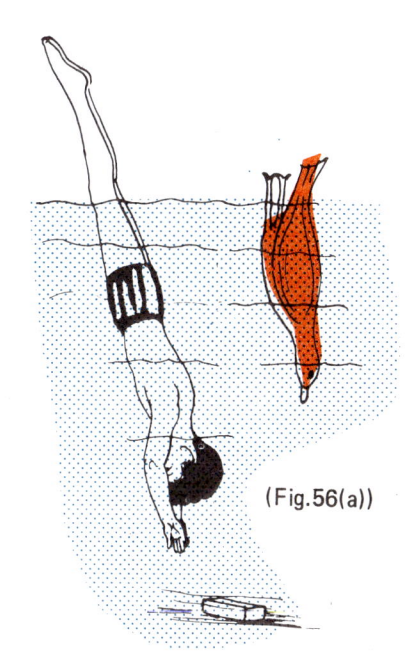

(Fig.56(a))

Jimmy's entry of surface dive and continuing surface dive

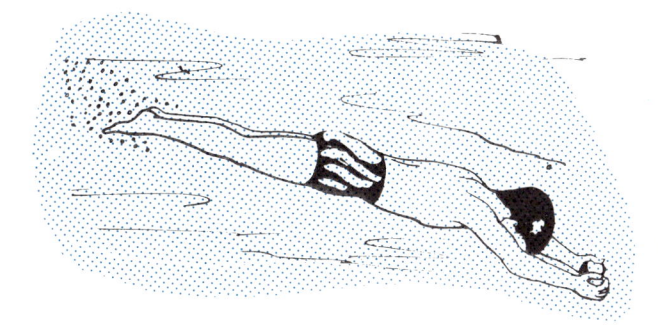

(Fig.56(b))

Picking up block

"After picking up the block, stand on the bottom of the bath, and push upward through the water". (Fig.57(a))

"Then swim on your back to the side of the bath, holding the block on your chest". (Fig.57(b))

Jimmy and Jenny were not very successful at first, mainly because they tried to pick up the block with one hand, with the result that the arm they had not straightened out in front of the head prevented them from getting down. However, by practising throwing their legs up straight and doing a kind of handstand down in the water, they got down easily to pick up the block with both hands. Then, as the block was moved further down the bath they were able to retrieve it in the deep end. If difficulty is experienced in getting down to the block, then swim downwards on breast stroke, open your eyes and look at the block to pick it up.

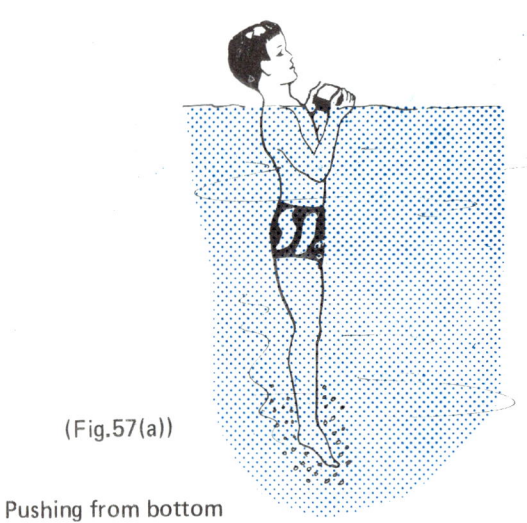

(Fig.57(a))

Pushing from bottom

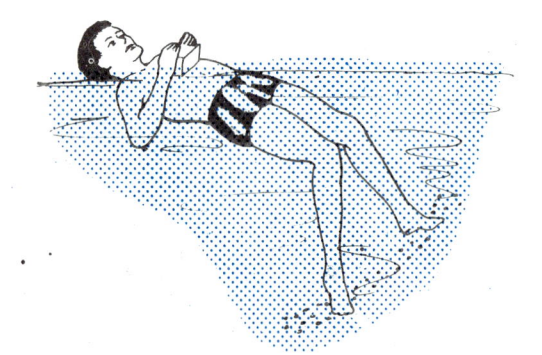

Holding block and swimming on life-saving kick

(Fig.57(b))

RESCUE METHODS — LIFE SAVING

Rescue by hand tow and chin carry.

I feel that this book would not be complete without reference to the saving of life from drowning together with the 'know-how' of applying emergency treatment to restore breathing after rescuing a person from the water.

I intend to limit my remarks to the simple and natural methods of rescue and resuscitation. The Royal Life Saving Society, in their illustrated handbook, deal with these subjects in a very efficient and admirable way, based on many years of actual and practical experience. I thoroughly recommend it to everyone; in fact, in view of the many fatalities that occur every year around our coast, in rivers and canals, this book should be a "must" in every home, school and library.

The most simple and effective method of rescue is the single handed clothes or chin method. (Fig.58 & 59.)

There is an old saying that a drowning person will clutch at any straw and I am sure that it is true, so the moral is: avoid a clutch if at all possible. For that reason, always try and approach a drowning person from behind or on the blind side. The following methods can then be used:

1. Take a firm grip of the clothing at the back of the person's neck and by using the other hand to assist in towing, make for the nearest landing spot.

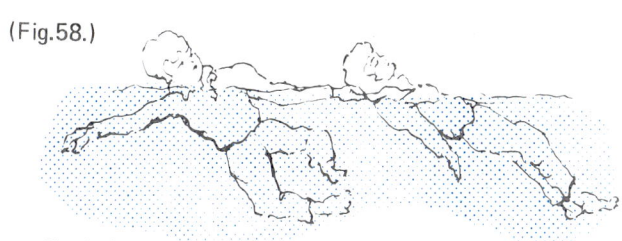

(Fig.58.)

Single hand tow, gripping clothing

or

2. Cup the hand under the person's chin and again using the free hand tow the person to land.

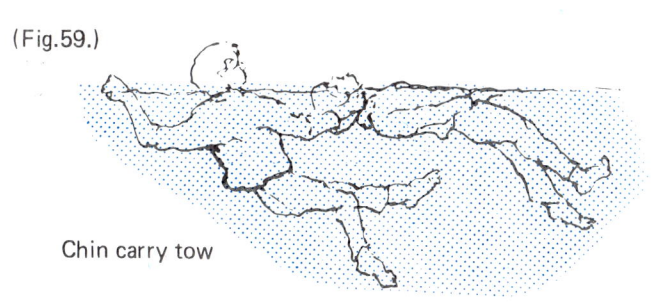

(Fig.59.)

Chin carry tow

Resuscitation — mouth to mouth or kiss of life

Having successfully brought the person to shore, the next thing, if the person is unconscious, is to revive him. The easiest and most effective way is the 'mouth to mouth' method, commonly known as the "kiss of life".

What to do

1. Tilt the head back, keeping one hand on the forehead and the other at the back of the neck as support. (Fig.60.)

2. Seal your mouth to the person's mouth and nose, blow air gently through the mouth to the lungs. Of course it will be necessary to take fresh intakes of air every few seconds and then repeat the exercise of blowing it through the mouth. (Fig.61(a)(b))

Between each blow of air, watch for the chest to rise and fall in order to know that air is inflating the lungs.

Stop when chest expands on its own.

Finally, having successfully accomplished a rescue, the most essential thing is to keep the person warm until more expert medical assistance can be obtained, and of course, in this day and age, dialling 999 for an ambulance is the quickest method of obtaining assistance.

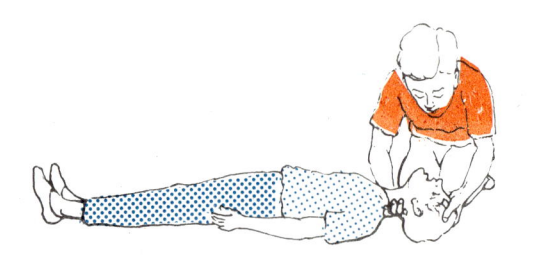

(Fig.60.)

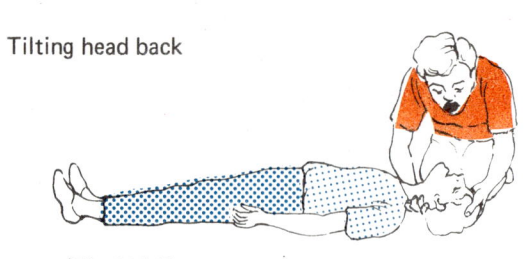

Tilting head back

(Fig.61(a))

Taking air prior to sealing mouth over nose and mouth

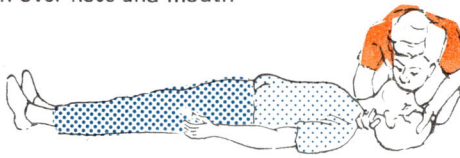

(Fig.61(b))

Blowing air into the mouth and lungs

Her Majesty The Queen (then Princess Elizabeth) together with Earl Mountbatten of Burma at the opening ceremony in London of The Earl Mountbatten medal Holders of The Royal Life Saving Society, when I received from Her Majesty my award as shown on page 60

The Royal Life Saving Society

Established 1891 Incorporated under Royal Charter 1924

Patron His Most Gracious Majesty The King
Vice Patron Her Royal Highness The Princess Elizabeth, Duchess of Edinburgh
President Vice-Admiral The Earl Mountbatten of Burma KG, PC, GCB, GCIE, GCVO, KCB, DSO

This is to Certify

that by Special Resolution confirmed at the Annual General Meeting held on

Saturday, June 2nd, 1961

Leonard Shearn, Esq., Bristol

was awarded the

Certificate of Thanks

In recognition of the very valuable services rendered to the Society by unremitting zeal in promoting and furthering its Aims and Objects.

Mountbatten of Burma — President
L. M. Churcher — Chairman Central Executive
Alwyn E. Bisco — Chief Secretary

The Royal Life Saving Society

Patron Her Majesty The Queen
Grand President Admiral of the Fleet the Earl Mountbatten of Burma
KG PC GCB GCSI GCIE GCVO DSO

This is to Certify

that by Resolution of the Commonwealth
Council of the Society

L. SHEARN

BRISTOL

was awarded the

SERVICE CROSS

In recognition of valuable services rendered
to the Society by unremitting zeal in
promoting its Aims and Objects

Chief Secretary

Mountbatten of Burma A.F.
Grand President

Debbie Adams of Bristol together with the A.S.A. President, Vice President, Secretary, Treasurer, Police Examiner and myself on a special occasion in London, when Debbie was awarded a solid gold Survival Award for being the millionth candidate to pass the test.

I taught Debbie from a beginner through all her swimming Awards.

BRONZE AWARD FOR PROFICIENCY IN PERSONAL SURVIVAL

SPONSORS:— Amateur Swimming Association

TESTS AND CONDITIONS

BRONZE AWARD: Dress: Men and Boys in trousers and shirt, or pyjamas; Women and Girls in dress, or slacks and blouse, or pyjamas.

1. Jump from a height of not less than 6 feet.
2. Swim 50 yards.
3. Tread water for 3 minutes in a vertical position.
4. Undress in the water.
5. Swim 440 yards, surface diving once during the swim, and swimming at least 5 yards completely submerged.
6. Climb out from deep water without the use of steps, or assistance. The level of the water must be at least 9 inches below the landing place.

SPECIAL CONDITIONS FOR HANDICAPPED PERSONS

The following special conditions may be applied at the discretion of the Examiner, or Examiners, who must certify on the examination report form that:—

"Candidates underlined have passed the examination subject to the special conditions numbered against their name, and I/We certify that they are so handicapped".

Conditions

A. BRONZE AWARD (for physically handicapped):—

1. Condition 1, delete "Jump" and substitute "Enter".
2. Condition 2, delete "in a vertical position".

Silver and Gold Awards are made by the Association for advanced standards of personal survival.

Organiser: Miss L.V. Cook, 12 Kings Avenue, Woodford Green, ESSEX. 1G8 0JB

Amateur Swimming Association –
English Schools' Swimming Association

JOINT
NATIONAL SWIMMING AWARDS
TESTS AND CONDITIONS

Stage 1

1. Jump, or make a head first entry, into the pool and swim continuously for two minutes using any stroke, or strokes, without contact with bath wall or floor.
2. Swim continuously for 50 yards using a recognised prone stroke.
3. Swim continuously for 50 yards by backstroke.

Stage 2

1. Dressed in: boys—pyjamas or trousers and shirt;
   girls—dress, or blouse and slacks, or pyjamas;
   jump or make a head first entry into the pool and swim continuously for 50 yards by any stroke or strokes.
2. Climb out of the bath or pool unaided and without use of steps, etc., and undress.
3. Surface dive from swimming, retrieve, carry and land an object, having swum with it a distance of not less than 8 yards.
4. Surface dive from swimming and swim not less than 5 yards under water.
5. Swim continuously for 200 yards using two different strokes with a minimum of 50 yards by any one stroke.

Organiser: Miss L.V. Cook, 12 Kings Avenue, Woodford Green, Essex, 1GB 0G8

Swimming stunts

To finally conclude, Mr. Wynne taught Jenny a Jimmy a few simple tricks to do in the water which they found very enjoyable.

The descriptions which follow are of Jenny doing "The Float" the "Forward Tuck Somersault" the "Backward Tuck Somersault" and "The Tub".

The Float

"First" said Mr. Wynne, "lie out on the surface of the water, keeping your legs relaxed and your knees very slightly bent, slowly take your arms back behind your head and keep breathing naturally". (Fig. 62 & 62(a))

Jenny showing "Float" (Front view) arms slowly going back. (Fig.62.)

Jenny showing the "Float" Side view (Fig.62(a))

65

Forward "Tuck" Somersault

Swim forward on the breast stroke, thrust your arms and head forward and downward in the same way as you did for your surface dive for the brick, and at the same time arch your back, tuck your knees up toward your chin and roll forward and over in the water. (Fig.63.)

This little trick will help considerably when it comes to practising the forward tumble turn in front crawl racing.

(Fig.63.)

Jenny showing "Forward tuck somersault"

Backward "Tuck" Somersault

Scull along the surface of the water then bring your knees up in front of you and as close as possible to your chin. Keep your knees tucked up and throw yourself backward and over into a complete somersault. (Fig.64 & 64(a))

You are halfway to doing the backward tumble turn in back crawl swimming when you can do this stunt.

(Fig.64.)

Jenny showing "Backward tuck somersault"

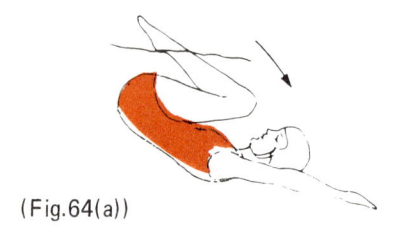

(Fig.64(a))

The Tub

Simply scull along the surface of the water and gently bring your knees up towards your chest. Keep your legs from your knees to the toes straight out on the surface of the water, and then by using the sculling action with your hands, swivel round and round, first one way and then the other. (Fig.65.)

These four stunts will also be of great value if at a future date you would feel desirous of joining a "Synchronised" swimming club and take part in its very attractive "Formation" swimming which is very popular in the U.S.A. and Canada, and making great strides in this Country, under the direction and driving force of Miss Helen Elkington, Technical Swimming Officer Amateur Swimming Association of Great Britain, F.I.S.T. and F.I.S.C.

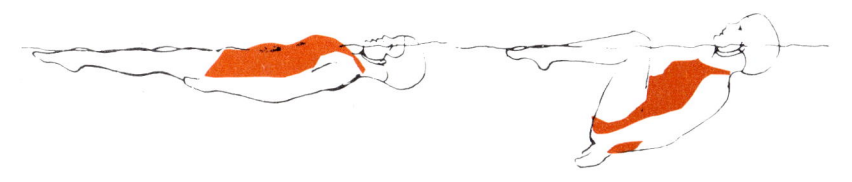

Jenny showing "The Tub"

(Fig.65.)

BRITISH SWIMMING COACHES ASSOCIATION

B.S.C.A., Station Hill, Bury St. Edmunds,
Suffolk IP32 6AD.
General Secretary: Philip Bennett.

The B.S.C.A. Badges as shown on pages 70 to 72 are open to all those swimmers who aspire to the times required, and all strokes must be in accordance with A.S.A. Laws.

25 yards
- Freestyle .... 18 secs.
- Backstroke .... 20 secs.
- Butterfly .... 21 secs.
- Breaststroke .... 22 secs.
- I.M. (4 x 25 yds.) .... 1m.40s.

$33\frac{1}{3}$ yards
- Freestyle .... 25 secs.
- Backstroke .... 28 secs.
- Butterfly .... 30 secs.
- Breaststroke .... 31 secs.
- I.M. (4 x $33\frac{1}{3}$ yds.) .... 2m.15s.

B.S.C.A. SPRINT SWIMMING AWARD — SILVER

50 yards
- Freestyle .... 35 secs.
- Backstroke .... 39 secs.
- Butterfly .... 42 secs.
- Breaststroke .... 45 secs.
- I.M. (4 x 25 yds.) .... 1m.30s.

66⅔ yards
- Freestyle .... 49 secs.
- Backstroke .... 55 secs.
- Butterfly .... 59 secs.
- Breaststroke .... 63 secs.
- I.M. (4 x 33⅓ yds.) .... 2m.00s.

B.S.C.A. SPRINT SWIMMING AWARD — GOLD

50 yards
- Freestyle .... 30 secs.
- Backstroke .... 35 secs.
- Butterfly .... 38 secs.
- Breaststroke .... 41 secs.
- I.M. (4 x 25 yds.) .... 1m.20s.

$66\frac{2}{3}$ yards
- Freestyle .... 42 secs.
- Backstroke .... 49 secs.
- Butterfly .... 53 secs.
- Breaststroke .... 58 secs.
- I.M. (4 x $33\frac{1}{3}$ yds.) .... 1m.46s.

THE ROYAL LIFE SAVING SOCIETY

UNITED KINGDOM

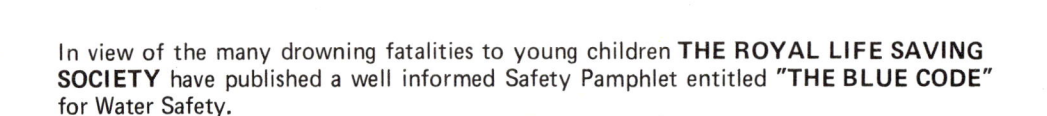

In view of the many drowning fatalities to young children **THE ROYAL LIFE SAVING SOCIETY** have published a well informed Safety Pamphlet entitled **"THE BLUE CODE"** for Water Safety.

The Society have kindly given me permission to encorporate this Safety Code in my book which is shown on pages 74 to 77.

If only **ONE** little life is saved, and I feel there will be many more, then all the effort put into this publication will be worth while.

POINTS TO REMEMBER

1. Swimming

* Never swim alone or when tired
* Wait at least an hour after a meal before swimming
* Don't show off
* Cold water can kill - get out as soon as you feel cold
* Take the advice of the lifeguards
* Don't take airbeds and inflatable toys into the sea
* At the seaside, check tide tables and ask what the local dangers are
* Swim in line with the shore
* Don't dive into unknown waters
* Don't wear goggles to dive other than when doing a racing dive
* If you need to wear goggles look for the kite mark

2. On the water

* Learn from the experts how to enjoy water sports safely
* Always wear a life-jacket
* Keep equipment in good working order
* Tell someone where you are going and when you will be back
* When boating wear warm clothing and non-slip footwear
* Never canoe alone
* Don't overload a boat
* Learn and Practise the capsize and man overboard drills
* Stay with a capsized boat

5. If someone else falls in

DON'T GO IN THE WATER

* Look for something to help pull him out (stick, rope, scarf), lie down so that you will not be pulled in too.
* If you cannot reach him, throw any floating object (rubber ring or ball) for him to hold on to, then FETCH HELP.

6. At home

* Watch toddlers at all times
* Cover fish ponds and pools with mesh
* Keep baths empty and bath plugs out of reach of small children
* Empty paddling pools when not in use

7. The 999 drill

You do **not** need coins to make an emergency call. The operator will answer a 999 call and ask:-

* 1. Which service you require
* 2. Your telephone number

You should ask for the **Police** (or the **Coastguard** if near the coast) The Police or Coastguard will then ask you:-

* 1. What the trouble is
* 2. Where it is
* 3. Whether anyone is capable of taking action while help is arriving
* 4. The telephone number you are speaking from
* 5. Your name and address

By knowing what the questions will be and being able to answer them you will speed the arrival of the emergency services

3. Out and about

* Report lifesaving equipment you see missing or anyone taking or breaking it
* Read and obey notices and never cover them up
* Keep away from disused gravel pits and quarries
* Watch out for slippery and crumbling river banks
* Never fish alone
* Keep a watchful eye on toddlers near water
* Keep off ice covered ponds, lakes or canals

4. If you fall in

* Keep calm
* Call for help
* Float on your back
* To attract attention wave one arm only

THE WATER SAFETY AWARD
WHAT YOU HAVE TO DO

Oral
Water Safety

Show a knowledge of water safety by answering questions from this code.

Practical
Basic Rescue

Demonstrate on land two methods of reaching someone in difficulties in the water using:-

    (1) a branch or length of wood

and (2) two articles of clothing tied together

Demonstrate on land throwing to **within reach** of a stationary subject over a distance of 6 metres:—

    (1) an unweighted rope

and (2) a large inflated ring or similar object

Resuscitation

Complete the basic test:-

Demonstrate to the satisfaction of the examiner the expired air method of resuscitation showing:-

    (a) the correct positioning of the subject

    (b) the mouth to nose technique

    (c) the mouth to mouth technique

    (d) action to be taken in case of

        (i) vomit

        (ii) recovery - placing the subject in the recovery position

How to take this Award

Information on how to undertake this Award is available from your nearest RLSS Awards Secretary — a current list can be obtained from:—

RLSS Headquarters
Mountbatten House
STUDLEY
Warwickshire
B80 7NN   (enclose SAE)

ADVANCED LIFESAVING

WATER SAFETY AWARD
It's a FIRST STEP on a wise journey

Reproduced with permission from "The Awards Schemes" (4th Edition 1978) R.L.S.S. Handbook Section 6, published by the Royal Life Saving Society — U.K.

From wheelchair to fitness through swimming

I have reserved the final true story to conclude my book, for two reasons. The first because of the complete satisfaction it gave me and secondly, and more important, because of the encouragement it will give to the handicapped and disabled.

It concerns Mrs. Dulcie Reed age 52 years, who came to me in a wheelchair, was paralysed from the hips down, and literally scared of the water. I leave her now to tell her own story which is as follows:-

49 Sunnyside Road,
Weston-super-Mare,
Somerset.

7th September, 1982

I had a stroke on the 17th January, 1967 which left me paralysed from the hips down with no movement or sensations. I was in hospital for 3 months where I was given therapy treatment and was discharged with a Zimmer and Tripod.

I was told that the best possible therapy was swimming. I had never been to a swimming bath in my life and was absolutely petrified of water. Someone told me about Mr. Shearn, so I went to him for swimming lessons at the Redwood Lodge Country Club, Bristol.

He put me at ease right away, worked very hard, and seemed to instil in me tremendous confidence. I worked very hard and that "slave driver" who called himself my "Instructor" made me work harder and harder. He kept me at it and miraculously I felt movement returning to my legs. The first time I had actual proof was when I kicked the wall of the swimming bath with my toe which made me shout "ooh".

Eventually, I have regained a good 75% of movement in both legs and I am able to go shopping, do my housework and tend my garden.

The amount of work necessary for my rehabilitation was tremendous, and I shall be forever grateful to swimming and to Mr. Shearn.

Dulcie L. Reed.